FREE AS A BIRD

In Memoriam: Lines On The Retirement Of Sir Richard 'Dickie' Bird

So. Farewell then
Dickie Bird.

Famous umpire.

With your white coat
And your
Cap.

You were a familiar figure
To cricket
Lovers.

'Over!'
That was your
Catchphrase.

Now it is.

E.J. Thribb (17½ not out).

With kind permission of Private Eye, *upon Dickie Bird's announcement of his retirement as a Test umpire, January 1996.*

FREE AS A BIRD

The Life and Times of
Harold 'Dickie' Bird

David Hopps

 Robson Books

For my Mother and Father

First published in Great Britain in 1996 by
Robson Books Ltd, Bolsover House,
5–6 Clipstone Street, London W1P 8LE

British Library Cataloguing in Publication Data
A catalogue record for this title is available from
the British Library

ISBN 1 86105 038 0

Typeset in Sabon by The Harrington
Consultancy, London
Printed and bound by Butler & Tanner Ltd,
Frome and London

Contents

Foreword by Geoffrey Boycott

SINCE becoming a first-class umpire in 1970, Dickie Bird has played God in front of us all, and I, for one, reckon he has played it rather well. There is no doubt in my mind that he has been the best umpire in the world. He has made very few mistakes and his mannerisms and eccentricity have allowed humour to develop in his relationships with players while never undermining his ability to control a game. When a Test match is in a tense situation, with batsmen and bowlers on edge, his ability to smooth over a situation has been second to none.

I have known many umpires over the years who have behaved too officiously. Dickie has never made that mistake. He has always been prepared to talk to players and build up a rapport. He has not been bound by the laws, but has interpreted them with a true feel for the game. He knows he possesses the authority and has not found cause to laud it over the players under his command.

Dickie has been like a good, old-fashioned community policeman, the sort who used to live in a local police house, drink in the local pub and play cricket for the local team. He has known his patch as well as anyone, sharing the players' world and understanding their fears and aspirations. He has loved his job, just as I used to love my batting. You can have the office, but that does not automatically bring you respect. Dickie has earned that respect, and that is something that money cannot buy. He has been fair, decent and honest, and his idiosyncrasies will always make you laugh.

I have known him since I was 13, when we were both making our way at Barnsley Cricket Club, and he has not changed a bit since then. Like me, he came from humble beginnings and he is at ease with that, never trying to hide it. He is just as comical and highly-strung now as he was then. Even when he was on the Yorkshire staff, he was still a nervous wreck when he batted for Barnsley. Before an innings, he would come up to me, shaking like a leaf, and exclaim: 'I can't get my gloves on, Gerald.' I would tell him that my name was Geoffrey and then give him a hand. When he had made 50, he would yell out from the middle for us to get the buckets ready for the collection before all the spectators went home. There I was, a 14- or 15-year-old kid, thinking that if this was what county cricket did for you, what chance had I got?

Dickie might have built friendships with players over the years, but there has never been a hint of bias. He never gave someone a decision just because they had been nice to him. At Yorkshire, I have seen some of our lads – players like Arnie Sidebottom and Graham Stevenson – trying to wind up Dickie. They would moan at him for not giving them a single decision and Dickie would get on his high horse, act as if he was flummoxed, and give them as good as he got. Some people who didn't understand him might have had their egos pricked, but he has a typically Northern humour. It is important not to take what he says too literally, to pick out what is part truth and what is said tongue in cheek.

Nowhere is that humour more obvious than in the scores of anecdotes that have tracked his career. Every story about Dickie is embellished to some degree, and he encourages it as much as anyone. He tells one about me, about how when he was invited to lunch, he had to break into Fortress Boycott by scaling a 10-foot wall and how all he got after all that was a toasted cheese sandwich. Well, I reckon he turned up unannounced, scaled a gate not a wall, and knew that I always have a light lunch.

But there is no malice in any Dickie Bird stories. He is welcome to see me any time. He has been a great umpire and deserves all the affection and respect that he is given.

Geoffrey Boycott OBE
Yorkshire and England
1996

1

Free As A Bird

'When I step across that boundary rope, I'm a different man. It's the only time I feel in total control'
— Dickie Bird

DICKIE Bird admits to leaping up in bed in the middle of the night, startled by aggressive fast bowlers yelling 'Howzat!' As recurring nightmares go, the world's most famous umpire has got off quite lightly. After all, he can always respond 'Not out,' and doubtless he invariably does. Why break the habit of a lifetime?

The time has now come for Bird to dream pleasanter dreams. His declaration that the Lord's Test between England and India in June 1996 would be his last signalled the end of one of the most cherished international careers in the history of the game. He was immediately lauded in the media as the fairest and most respected umpire in history. Which present-day cricketer could rival the popularity of Dickie Bird as he dabbed his eyes and prepared to walk out at Lord's in a Test for the last time? Certainly, no Englishman would come close. Sachin Tendulkar and Brian Lara are as famous, and Tendulkar, in particular, is held in great esteem throughout India. But neither can outdo the worldwide popularity of the twitching, fussing and cuff-shooting Yorkshireman in the white cap.

He retires as one of the most beloved, proficient and eccentric figures of his sporting generation: a kindly man traipsing comically through a never-ending succession of minor disasters. He might have been described as the Norman Wisdom of the umpiring circuit (both, after all, favoured similarly shaped caps) if it wasn't for the fact that he has been a sight funnier than Wisdom ever was.

His decision was all the more praiseworthy because – with a little help from his friends – he recognised that the time was right for him to go. He had the good sense to stand down at Test level while his stock was still high, before murmurs and hints about deteriorating judgement turned into more hurtful criticism. We should all be grateful to him for that.

'I don't think anybody in his sixties can be as good as when he was in his forties,' he said. 'I wanted to go out at the top and retire with dignity. I didn't want people to say that Dickie Bird was slipping.'

His timing ensured that he departed with his dignity intact, although to stop the rumbles that his judgement was on the wane, he would have had to retire from Test match cricket slightly earlier. There had been mutterings from his umpiring colleagues, from players under his command and from the media. Dickie, the feeling went, was not the supreme judge that he used to be. But he was an institution and institutions are not jettisoned lightly, especially in English cricket, where history and tradition are treated with overriding respect. No sport is more besotted with its past.

When great players retire, our sadness is alleviated by a sense of inevitability. We all come to learn that youth does not last for ever, and we recognise the greater distress involved in watching our sporting heroes cling on long after their talents have started to wane. But umpires ... dammit – aren't they meant to endure for ever? A slightly arthritic hobble to square leg, the endless stretching of a bad back, become not so much a sign of weakness as part of their charm. It doesn't take that much energy to raise a finger. That their faculties have waned too far catches us almost by surprise.

Bird's intention was to serve out his time until compulsory retirement at 65 on the county circuit, an extensive farewell tour awash with appreciative applause, from the Panama-brimmed pensioners lolling in the Hove deckchairs to a few well-meant grumbles from the demanding and dogmatic members in front of the Old Trafford pavilion. He could also anticipate a few scornful hoots and hollers whenever he dared to peer at his light meter, especially if he did so at Headingley where they have long blamed him for every dark cloud that happens to let loose its load over Leeds 6. Not that Bird would be too concerned. After the trials and tribulations of the last 25 years, nothing on his farewell tour was likely to cause him to wake up in a cold sweat. Not unless he got another chance to meet the Queen, or someone in authority decided to follow up the MBE he was awarded in 1986 with a knighthood.

Bird invests his presentation of the MBE at Buckingham Palace with almost childlike delight and regards it as the outstanding memory of his career. He often says it means more to him than his life. When he received it the Queen was moved to ask why he was crying. He was nearly as overwhelmed the following day, when an Old Trafford crowd applauded him onto the field. 'There I was, a Yorkshireman, at Lancashire's headquarters, receiving a standing ovation,' he blurted.

He has always been a faithful devotee of the establishment, which might go some way to explaining why the establishment, beginning with the Test and County Cricket Board, have been so supportive towards him.

'I am very much an establishment man – I turned down Kerry Packer and the South African Breweries tour – and to be honoured by the Queen meant everything to me,' he has admitted. 'I was crying when she handed it over to me and I had to apologise to her because I was so proud.'[1]

'She said: "Dickie, are you umpiring in the Lord's Test tomorrow?" I said I was and she said: "I'll be there to see you on Friday, then." Fantastic. The Queen Mother has also been wonderful to me. In the Queen's Jubilee year she invited the umpires and the players from the England/Australia Test out to Clarence House and she said to me: "Dickie, you haven't been wearing your white cap today." I said that was because it had been overcast and I hadn't needed it. She said: "I always know it's you when I see that white cap and all those twitches." Money can't buy that, you know.'[2]

The establishment has occasionally found Bird's style a little grating, but they have always been grateful for his unquestioning loyalty. Sir Gubby Allen, a massively influential figure at Lord's until his death in 1989, was known to remark on occasion: 'He's a damn fine umpire, but I must have a word with him about all this fussing around.' Others privately wondered whether his repetitive use of the word 'Sir' was charmingly old-fashioned or a mite toadying. No matter. However panic-stricken Bird might sometimes have appeared, especially when rain and bad light threatened, those in authority knew that his fidelity was as constant as a favourite family pet. His deference to authority seems almost to hark back to the Victorian age.

So intent was he on not offending the great and the good that his obsessive timekeeping became legendary. He arrived absurdly early for drinks at Downing Street with Mrs Thatcher, early for lunch at Chequers with John Major, and early for dinner at Buckingham Palace with the Queen. As Sue Lawley had the good sense to ask on *Desert Island Discs*: 'Why? It's very embarrassing, isn't it?' The only possible answer is that he does it to stave off the minor calamities that are always lurking around the next corner. (His choice of music on *Desert Island Discs* revealed many basic truths about him: 'Abide With Me'

for a man of strong religious faith; Barbra Streisand's 'The Way
We Were' for an unashamed romantic regularly given to tears;
'Land Of Hope And Glory' for a fervent royalist; and Nat King
Cole's 'When I Fall In Love' in memory of a love affair in the
early 1960s that was forsaken for his greater commitment to
the game of cricket.)

I was fortunate enough to write a few pages of this book in
the Bentota Beach Hotel, in Sri Lanka, where the country's
idyllic west coast beaches are at their finest. A tea waiter
discovered why I was tapping away four-fingered at a lap-top
computer rather than doing what everybody else was doing:
surfing, sunbathing, snorkelling or speedboating. It became
impossible to leave the room without being greeted by half the
hotel staff chortling 'Dickie Bird, Dickie Bird,' and adopting
manic expressions as they pointed their index fingers to the
heavens. After half an hour of this treatment, I was exhausted
and needed a lie down. Quite how Dickie has coped with such
attention for all these years is impossible to imagine.

It is at such times that one reminds oneself that Dickie Bird
is only an umpire, for heaven's sake, a man charged simply
with providing the orderly environment in which the players
themselves can flourish. Yet Bird himself has won extraordinary affection, while many players, hidden behind helmets,
protective grilles, sunglasses or sunhats, seem to lack the
character and individuality that make cricket the most appealing and enriching of sports. He is a wonderful bonus in a more
soulless age.

Matthew Engel, editor of *Wisden Cricketers' Almanack*,
asserts: 'What has been so welcome about Dickie is that he has
been an instantly identifiable figure on a cricket field at a time
when most players are no longer as identifiable. It is not only
that batsmen wear helmets. There is more pressure to conform,
more of a football mentality surrounding the game. Coaches
are stressing the team ethic, sometimes at the expense of
allowing individuality to flourish. The fact that there is more
money in the game also encourages a greater seriousness.

'Furthermore, as cricket requires ever greater athleticism, it is increasingly becoming a younger man's game. No-one can expect players in their early twenties to overflow with as much character as would be the case much later in their career. They have simply not lived long enough. The first-class game has lost those much-loved figures who played for 20 or 30 seasons until their mid-forties. They became part of first-class cricket's fabric. Jack Hobbs, for instance, hit 100 hundreds after the age of 40; it is inconceivable that that will ever happen again.

'Now careers at the top are much shorter. It is harder for players to develop a character with which the public can identify. Dickie has, to some extent, been a substitute. In that way there is no doubt that he has been very good for the game. Mums know who he is, far more so than they might recognise the England new-ball attack. Perhaps it is very sad that we have reached a stage where the umpires are the characters – we would all rather be talking about the players – but at least it is something. Dickie will be remembered with affection for a long, long time.'

What the world sees and values in Dickie Bird above all else is an essential humanity. There is no side to him, no threat, no hidden agenda. A less dissembling man would be almost impossible to imagine. His umpiring has been virtuous and scrupulously fair, even if he has often needed the assistance of his colleagues to get him through the day in one piece. His humour, in fact his whole lifestyle, is as mild and inoffensive as the Ealing comedies of the 1950s. He is living proof that good guys can win.

A player burdened by the stresses of a Test match, fearing personal failure, and so wrapped up in his own game that he begins to suspect that he, alone, is stricken by nerves, can see Bird's own agitation, as he natters away reminding himself to concentrate on every ball, and feel comforted by it.

Bird has always shown great sympathy towards the players under his wing. As someone who struggled to make an impression with Yorkshire and Leicestershire, he is keenly aware of the agonies of failure. David Graveney, general secretary of the Cricketers' Association, gives a lovely tongue-in-cheek rendition of how, in his years as a left-arm spinner, he would occasionally tire of being struck for six to the sound of Dickie assuring him that he had been very, very unfortunate and that it was by far the best ball he had bowled that over.

Occasionally, however, when he is at his most jittery, a player's failure has been transformed, in Bird's mind, into his own personal disaster. Peter Roebuck, a former Somerset captain and now cricket correspondent of *The Sunday Times*, recognises this: 'What typifies Dickie is the way, when someone drops a simple caught-and-bowled, that he goes off to square leg convinced that the error will become his own personal disaster. A caught-and-bowled, after all, would have been a simple decision, taking place right under his nose. What will happen now is that he will get a close lbw decision, or an appeal for the faintest edge, or a run-out that comes down to a couple of inches. Anything that is going to make his life a nightmare. He has had a lugubrious way of anticipating impending disaster and, as such, it inevitably arises.'

Dickie likes a moan. Walking out for the start of a Lord's Test against the West Indies, he was once heard to exclaim: 'Here we go, five days of bloody purgatory.' Umpiring colleagues who prefer a quiet life have occasionally made the same joke about him.

Players, for the most part, have been glad to see him because they trust him implicitly and because he has made them laugh. For five months every summer, the county circuit is a treadmill where players struggle to maintain their freshness and enthusiasm in the face of ever-increasing burdens. It can be a thankless task. Bird offers them the chance of light relief.

Spectators adore Bird because he fills their day with colour, transforming every minor incident into a full-scale melodrama. If the game is dull there is always the chance that Bird's shins will accidentally intervene to stop a searing straight drive, or that he will be tormented by a pigeon which chooses to alight in mid-pitch. Even on the most uneventful of days there is always something to put him into a flap. The media also welcome him for much the same reason. He has always been approachable, and even if half-an-hour of fluster leaves no-one any the wiser as to the issue at hand, there will always be a funny story to relate on the return to the press box. For a profession which learns to live with arrogant officials or distrusting players, his complete absence of pomposity does him tremendous credit.

His pride in his profession is both impressive and endearing. There may have been times when his fellow umpires have longed for such a senior figure to fight for their rights more strenuously. Bird, though, has never been a politician. Wait for him to approach the TCCB and demand a pay rise and you will wait for ever. But his loyalty to his profession, and to members of it worldwide, is unequivocal. 'I will defend umpires against anyone,' he says. 'They are all fair and honest men doing their best.'

He is proud of his achievements, but that does not mean that he is conceited or arrogant. In any case, such undisguised pride has a refreshing simplicity, and can seem preferable to the false modesty which has become a British character trait.

As his umpiring career developed, he would habitually respond to each major appointment by telephoning a series of Yorkshire newspapers. On-duty reporters would pick up the phone to be informed in booming South Yorkshire tones: 'Dickie Bird, international umpire from Barnsley 'ere. Ah've bin appointed to stand in't Lord's Test in June. It's my xth Test, and ah thought you'd like to mention it.' It was an uncustomary way of going about things, but nobody questioned his display of self-esteem, because, well, Dickie was Dickie, and one could appreciate his excitement and the unconcealed pride in his voice.

He has been more universally accepted than other famous Yorkshire cricketers of recent vintage. Geoffrey Boycott has been a much misunderstood man, but there has been a caustic and tactless edge to his character that has not always endeared him to his friends and has given his enemies a field day. Raymond Illingworth, as England's chairman of selectors, has been both frank and knowledgeable, but operating against that has been a stubbornness which can make him overly dismissive of other people's opinions. Then there is Fred Trueman, a fast bowler in his heyday of enormous skill and potency, but a man whose scathing criticism of modern-day players makes him sound like his own *Spitting Image* puppet.

All three, great players that they were, committed lovers of the game, present 'Yorkshireness' as dogmatic, inflexible and opinionated. 'So what's new?' many of those born outside those broad acres might ask. But there is another type of Yorkshireness, a guileless and straightforward way of life, in which friendships are valued and behaviour is sincere and unfeigned. It is those qualities that have been exemplified by Dickie Bird.

There is another facet of Bird's personality that is equally endearing – his gratitude to the game. Cricket has enabled him to live a successful, satisfying and productive life and he has never been slow to give thanks. As Peter Roebuck puts it: 'He has never exploited the game; he needed the game. He was a character who made the game grow and who grew himself because of the game. In some umpires, you can see a weariness, or a popularism or a cynicism. Dickie was never afflicted by any of those.'

To show such unreserved appreciation of his opportunities is largely out of kilter with modern-day attitudes throughout professional sport, where a depressing number of competitors assume that the game owes them a living, that the fans should be grateful for their very presence, and that the media are parasites that they could best do without. As the development of players intensifies, as it must if England are to become successful again, the danger is that those whose potential is identified from an early age will be thrown into representative matches before they have had a chance to develop a true appreciation of the game. In England, the enthusiasm of professional players is further worn down by an overloaded domestic programme which promotes quantity above quality to the detriment of the international side.

Maximising their own income – in the form of Test appearances, sponsorship deals or benefit years – to help them offset a disturbingly early retirement inevitably becomes an obsession for many English players. How many of them can honestly say that they are still playing because of a love for the game? Those who can respond 'yes,' with no hesitation, should be cherished.

The most striking aspect of England's failure in the 1996 World Cup was that they failed to communicate any sense of enjoyment. They had become worn down by a surfeit of cricket. International cricket had become a job, and enforced overtime at that. As defeat followed defeat, to some it was close to drudgery. The logical case (if not the emotional one) for restructuring English domestic cricket seemed inescapable.

Compare that state of mind with the World Cup winners, Sri Lanka, whose *joie-de-vivre* was a delight, who revelled in every contest, and who still retained a recognition of the wonderful opportunities that cricket had given them. A country that has maintained its humour throughout a long civil war is not about to moan about the hardship of playing cricket. They still value the sense of opportunity.

Dickie Bird possesses exactly that type of attitude, a blissful appreciation of the benefits that cricket has given him. It is hard to imagine that he could ever become jaded or cynical. He seeks no release from a game that constantly fulfils him. Some might dismiss this as naive, but theirs is the sad attitude, not his. Who does not yearn, at some time or other, for an ability to savour life's simple pleasures? Where cricket is concerned, Bird has always had that gift, sharing in the emotional highs and lows of every cricketer who has played under his wing. Bird cares when a great innings falls just short of its target, and sympathises with a fine spell of bowling that goes unrewarded. And because, in his benign and guileless way, he communicates his joy to all of us, we identify with him all the more.

And then, most importantly, he makes us laugh. Bird's eccentricity is the stuff of legend and has led him into a bewildering number of ludicrous episodes, many of which will be relived in later chapters. But for all the practical jokes that have been played against him, or all the madcap behaviour that has been part and parcel of his life, his umpiring skills have consistently been held in the highest regard. He has always commanded respect from the players under his wing.

For eccentricity and authority to go together is rare enough. To combine them in such quantity as Bird has is arguably unique. His fussing around has rarely fostered disrespect, but has helped to create a congenial and supportive environment in which players can rise above the tension of a big occasion. Only in cricket, where even the shortest contest unfolds over most of a day, could such a style bring so much success. Football or rugby referees showing such idiosyncrasies would never be tolerated; these are more hectic games, intolerant of such fripperies. But cricket, at its best, fosters character and, even in the most intense contest, allows space for a display of humanity.

'I do fuss around, trying to be human, sharing the tension with the players,' he has explained. 'I know how uptight they can feel out there and it's important to me that they hold me in respect. I talk to all of them out on the field.'[3]

In his ability to keep the peace in the most heated circumstances, Bird's body language has been crucial. It is entirely non-confrontational. He is forever ready to be compassionate, a man searching for empathy. In terms of the prison officers in the BBC comedy *Porridge,* he has been Mr Barrowclough on the surface, but with a touch of Mr Mackay underneath. If he wags a finger, he does so not just in stern admonishment of a player for a criminal act, but in horror-struck confusion over why that player should have miscalculated by behaving badly. The suggestion is not that the player will live to regret his transgressions as much as the fact

that Bird himself will become a broken man. Few players want
that on their conscience. Spared an officious ticking-off, which
might only have caused more resentment, the player instead
becomes mildly embarrassed by Bird's obvious distress and is
normally grateful when offered the chance to abandon his
grouse and get on with the game. Bird's fussing seems to say to
the perpetrator, you are not only angering me, but you are
hurting me. How can you behave like this? I know that you
have far too much appreciation of the game to act in this way.
Sort yourself out, and I'll forgive you. The last thing you want
to do is make an even greater mistake. And, time after time,
forgiveness is sought and granted, and the game reverts to its
contented atmosphere of old. Bird appeals to something that
many social commentators feel is declining in British society,
with damaging consequences; he appeals to a person's sense of
shame.

To emphasise one essential difference between cricket and
football, it is worth pointing out that when Dennis Lillee, the
Australian fast bowler, playfully pinched Bird's cap and wore it
himself on one occasion at the Oval, Dickie's shoulders shook
with laughter. Compare that with the outcome of an equally
light-hearted escapade by Paul Gascoigne, the Rangers and
England footballer, in a Scottish League match in the 1995/6
season. When Gascoigne picked up a referee's yellow card and
jokingly brandished it at him, the referee took umbrage, took
the card, and booked him. There is no doubt which is the more
humane game.

Lillee, for one, is shrewd enough to recognise that not every
umpire could operate in Bird's style, nor would the players
welcome it. His natural eccentricity has led to an individualistic
style which it would be disastrous for his fellow umpires to try
to copy.

Umpiring is a position of power, but Bird has never found
that one of its main attractions. Forty years ago David
Sheppard, an England opening batsman (and today the Bishop
of Liverpool) went as far as to suggest: 'Umpires do the job

because of their lust for power.' As a Christian man, he would doubtless concede that the most famous representative of the breed over the past 25 years has finer and more interesting motives.

Michael Parkinson once memorably described Bird as 'a lightning conductor for misfortune'. It has often seemed that way, although there has been some tendency towards exaggeration. At times, England's favourite umpire has not been averse to revelling in his image. But as well as retreating into a comforting world of well-worn stories, Bird also possesses a natural comic talent. Parkinson has written: 'The man you see on television, the twitchy, careworn, fraught individual with head bowed against the troubles of the world, is only a part of the whole being. There is a lot of laughter in him.' In his constant anxiety, he may mutter away for several minutes to little purpose and then, just when everyone is beginning to despair, he demonstrates his extraordinary capacity to bring laughter. It is often because his innocent view of the world seems slightly askew to reality.

One exchange with Helena De Bertodano, in *The Sunday Telegraph*, shortly after he announced his retirement from international cricket, is a masterpiece. Dickie, in typically agitated fashion, was detailing his early arrival for a lunch date with the Prime Minister, John Major.

'"I was supposed to be at Chequers at 12 o'clock and somehow I got there at 9.30, so the police rang John Major and he said: 'If it's Dickie, then send him through.' So I went and sat with John and Norma for two-and-a-half hours, nattering about cricket." '

'Didn't John Major have to run the country that morning, I ask?

'"Oh no," exclaims Dickie. "It was a Sunday, you see."'[4]

Life is that mild for Dickie Bird: trains still puff clouds of white smoke, there is always jam and scones for tea, and prime ministers always take Sundays off.

Bird is a habitual worrier, a man perfectly capable of acting as his own alarm clock. He never leaves the house without fretting whether he has locked the door or turned the lights off. Overseas journeys disturb him even more – he was once sceptical about fulfilling a tour of India because of his fear of pneumonic plague. No more restless man has ever trod a cricket field; he has imagined disaster lurking in the most innocent areas. Will that streak of cirrus cloud blowing away to the west suddenly howl towards him, transform itself into a scowling mass of cumulo-nimbus and drench him to the skin? By teatime will the superficial mark on a length at the pavilion end have deteriorated into a crack so wide and spiteful that the pitch will become unplayable? Is God going to insist that he has to turn down another lbw appeal before lunchtime? Will the frayed pocket of his umpiring coat become a large hole through which he will assuredly lose all his counters?

Real disasters attach themselves to him, too, or at least they seem to. Leaking drains, sunshine reflecting off greenhouses, bomb scares in the middle of a Lord's Test match, and streakers running all over his pitch are just a few of the episodes that have plagued him. He has been so fated by rain and bad light that it would have been no surprise if he had decided to travel around the first-class circuit by Ark.

To problems all and sundry, he responds as tormentedly as an old fishwife whose honour has been impugned. Metaphorically at least, he hitches up his skirt with a hammed-up expression of outrage and then witters and waves away his troubles until a proper sense of decorum is re-established. As Bird has dithered over disasters real and imaginary, his repertoire of nervous habits has become ever greater. The one that characterises him most is his agitated pumping forward of the arms. Many hours have been wasted wondering what he might be doing. Some imagine that he is revving up a motorbike, but that seems too daredevil for Dickie. Much more preferable to believe that he is winding up a washing line, back in his own back garden in South Yorkshire.

There is a host of other gestures, too. The slightest

complication causes him to brush the palm of his hand across his nose and over a fevered brow as if his world has collapsed around him. The amount of stress he is undergoing can be measured by means of the 'tug factor': tugs at the sleeves and tail of his umpire's jacket, tugs at his cap, tugs at his trousers. In the latter stages of his career, he has refused an appeal not merely by standing still, but by slapping one hand deep into his pocket and pressing the other into the small of his back so fiercely that it would be no surprise if it drilled through his stomach and emerged at the other side. Even on the coldest day, Bird cannot be without a handkerchief, which he uses repeatedly to mop his brow whenever tension begins to rise. In his younger days, nothing was more recognisable than a rapid scuttle away from the wicket like a fearful crab.

Waving away the Oval pigeons from mid-pitch was a task that, under Bird's charge, could become a midsummer pantomime. Not that many people minded; one TV clip of such an incident reveals the batsman on strike, David Gower, not bemoaning his loss of concentration but smiling at the whole affair. It all added to the fun of the occasion and reminded players, often at moments of great tension, that it was only a game.

Bird has also been hit by the ball so often, or nearly hit, or nearly hit only in his own imagination, that nobody could fail to foresee the melodrama that assuredly followed: the exaggerated, stage-managed limp, a feigned glare and gesture at the offending batsman, the imploring of the fielding side for a spot of sympathy, a brief fit of giggles and, in conclusion, the realisation that it was time to pull himself together and encourage everyone to get on with the game. It was a comic routine as well known as any in the land, and the crowd lapped it up every time.

Equally endearing has been the huge grin which breaks to the surface upon the fall of a wicket, partly a recognition of a bowler's talent, but also the brief release of tension which might have built up over several overs, an entire session, or even most of the day. Bird could be seen smiling broadly when Shane Warne dismissed Salim Malik during the Hobart Test between Australia and Pakistan in late 1995. As Warne had accused Salim Malik of trying to bribe him to throw a Test in Pakistan the previous winter, and there were some old scores to settle, such a smile could have been given an unfortunate interpretation. Had an Australian umpire grinned like that, it might have had damaging ramifications. But not with Dickie; he was smiling out of pleasure at the culmination of a contest. Nobody ever imagined otherwise. His integrity was eternally taken as read.

Bird's emotions habitually run near the surface. He is dragged this way and that by the forces of laughter, tears and worry. The day he announced that his farewell Test would be at Lord's, he shed a tear or two in anticipation, and continued to shed them as the weeks progressed. He invested the occasion with as much drama as a royal wedding. Such were the expectations of the floods of tears that would follow when the day finally arrived that the Lord's groundstaff would have been best advised to have a line of whales on stand-by to mop up the water. Imagine the headlines: 'Tears Stop Play'.

It is difficult to think of a sporting personality more intoxicated by tears than Dickie. A farewell Test at Lord's, a happy word from the Queen Mother and, increasingly as he gets older, the regret that he has never had a son to call his own are just three subjects designed to tug his heartstrings. In the country of the stiff-upper-lip (and that can be putting it kindly) his waves of emotion can be quite off-putting, leading his detractors to suggest he is play-acting. But he has been this way all his life. Just imagine what he would have been like if he had been born Italian.

Dickie Bird is grateful to the game because he recognises that it has moulded him. Outside cricket, he has little to identify him. He has never married or experienced any deep and lasting emotional relationship outside his family. His friendships are wedded to the game. He has no other outside interest, apart from perhaps a casual interest in football. There have been few suggestions that his thoughts – or even his regrets – ever stray into other areas. He is a loyalist and a monarchist, but by nature rather than evaluation. He is not one to question life. His curiosity stretches little further than cricket folk, cricket memories, cricket talk, and cricket scores. He has been entirely sustained by the sport he loves.

'I'm the type of bloke who never questions anything,' he has often admitted.

He is remorseful about little that he has not done, only about something that he did do and he wishes he had not. Bird, the loyal Yorkshireman, regrets that he ever left his native county to join Leicestershire. It was arguably one of the most courageous decisions of his life, when he recognised that his future at Yorkshire was limited and he had the presence of mind to strike out elsewhere. But he is proud of his White Rose county and he is quick to surrender to the mists of nostalgia. An unabashed romantic is Dickie.

He routinely arrives at cricket grounds before anybody else (often three hours before the start of a Test match), partly because he wants to ensure that no detail is left to chance, partly because he has nothing much else to do. He does not ask for much in the hours before a match, other than a nearby toilet which he is apt to visit frequently as the nerves begin to bite. Extended sessions put an awful strain on his bladder, especially if he has had to withstand a couple of streakers and a Mexican wave. He has suspended at least one Test – England v West Indies at Old Trafford in 1984 – so that he could scurry off to the toilet.

He has toyed with the idea of becoming a match referee after his retirement, and his umpiring colleague John Hampshire thinks he would do the job well. But it is unlikely that the ICC would ever contemplate taking the risk. They prefer their match referees to strive for a certain gravitas. When it comes to exuding an air of calm authority, Dickie Bird, for all his undoubted qualities, would not come in the top one million.

Recall Clive Lloyd's masterful performance in the 1996 World Cup semi-final, when Sri Lanka were on the brink of victory against India and the Calcutta crowd caused the game to be abandoned as they flung bottles onto the outfield and lit fires on the terraces. Lloyd emphasised his authority from the start. Invested with the necessary powers, he dared to use them and the game surely benefited as a result. Now picture dear old Dickie in the same situation. 'What should I do, what should I do?' he would fuss and fret. He would strive to be fair, exceedingly so, but they might still be there now. Simply, the situation warrants a different type of authority than the kind he has shown on the field. Perhaps he will prove otherwise – and, if he does, the best of British – but it is doubtful that he will ever be given the chance.

Bird has shown an impressive self-awareness in admitting his fears about his retirement. He will be the showman without a show to go to. 'What worries me is that if I sit [at home],' he said, 'I will just worry myself away. I'd be dead within 12 months.'[5]

Within the game Bird will be valued and remembered for generations. Remove cricket and he can cut a solitary figure, unequipped to cope in a harsh and demanding world. He is a single man who rarely cooks for himself and who is grateful that his sister, Marjorie, pops in regularly to do his household chores. Even after more than 25 years on the county circuit he can still agonise over which route to take between grounds, journeys which by now he should be able to do in his sleep. The anxieties that, on the field, have contributed to the nation's affection, threaten off the field to consume him.

Dickie Bird recognised from the start that many people thought he would never make the grade as an umpire.

'They said, "There is no way that Dickie will make it as an umpire because he worries so much. He's just a bag of nerves." I knew what they meant. I've always been highly strung, always had that twitch with the arms. And before a match I still have to go to the toilet three or four times because of my nerves. Off the field, I'm a born worrier. But when I step across that boundary rope, I'm a different man. It's the only time I feel in total control.'

Such an admission he has made more than once, and it invites concern for his future. Without cricket, who knows what would have happened to him? By his own admission, a man who, however fleetingly, has touched the hearts of millions might have struggled to cope with his life. Instead of the widespread popularity he has earned, his nervousness might have tempted him to become an increasingly neurotic and withdrawn figure.

Life without cricket might have proved a bewildering, caged existence for such a warm-hearted, innocuous man. Fortunately, it never came to that. Cricket has been his salvation, enabling him to live a fruitful and rewarding life. For most of his years, he has been largely dependent upon it. It has provided a framework of laws and moral certainties that he understands. It has given him entertainment and excitement. It has allowed him to feel in absolute control. Quite simply, whenever he has walked out onto a cricket field, he has felt as *Free As A Bird*.

2

All of a Flap

'Umpiring at the top now is full of comedians and gimmicks. In the old days there used to be men you could respect' – Cec Pepper, resigning from the first-class umpiring list in 1980

WHEN Dickie Bird was reported to have announced on the field of play during England's 1995 Test series against the West Indies that he had 'lost his marbles', there were some who joked that it was an overdue admission of insanity. That the world's most famous Test umpire was merely undergoing another minor calamity – he had allegedly misplaced the miniature red barrels with which he records the number of balls in an over – turned out to be a bit of an anticlimax.

'Great bloke, completely bonkers,' said Ian Botham of the finest umpire in the game, and few would care to argue. His quirkiness is part of his charm.

Bird has commanded respect while happily exhibiting the more bizarre side of his personality. In extolling his virtues, no-one seeks to disguise the fact that his eccentricity is unrivalled among those who have reached the pinnacle of their sporting profession.

Barrie Leadbeater, the former Yorkshire batsman, whose first first-class match was alongside Bird in 1981, has maintained an unwavering respect for his colleague, but recognises, too, that Bird possesses an insecurity often seen in a great clown. He desperately wants to be liked.

'Dickie is so loyal,' Leadbeater said. 'He'd be distraught if you thought anybody disliked him. His antics can stretch people's patience at times, but there is not an ounce of ill-will in him.'

To seek to unravel every last ounce of truth and fiction in the wealth of comic anecdotes that have tracked his career is a futile task worthy of several misplaced lifetimes. When Bird himself is in full swing, fondly relating another extraordinary episode, exact details tend to be overlooked in his relish for a good story. Even an audience with the Queen – and he idolises nobody more, unless it is the Queen Mother – can sound like wonderful fantasy in Bird's hands. At Wakefield, the train is delayed especially for him because he has left his tickets in the car; arriving five hours early for his appointment, he whiles away several hours in a coffee shop near Buckingham Palace; when he does arrive at lunch unscathed, he frets about, cutting the grapes with a pair of scissors and they finish up all over the floor.

Note, too, that every character in the story has a punchline. The guard at Wakefield station mutters: 'I'll 'old t'train for you, Dickie, but ah wudden 'old it fer tha mate, Boycott.' The policeman outside Buckingham Palace has a choice of lines. Sometimes he exclaims: 'You're a bit early, we haven't had the changing of the guard yet.' Occasionally, by way of variation, there is a spot of repartee:

Policeman: 'Go and have a cup of coffee.'

Dickie (exasperatedly): 'But I've got four hours to kill!'

Policeman (patiently): 'Well, have two cups of coffee then.'

And when 'one of the happiest days of [his] life' continues with him dropping the grapes all over a Buck House carpet, even the Queen pipes up, as if on cue: 'Don't worry, Dickie, the corgis will look after them.' They do, too, eating up every last one. 'Perhaps these things always happen,' Dickie likes to wonder at this stage, a man forever living in hope. It is an umpiring life as told by Galton and Simpson, and it is wonderful stuff.

Michael Parkinson, a keen observer of Bird for nearly 50 years, also emphasises his mode of delivery. 'When he is telling a favourite anecdote, Mr Bird stands up. When he does so he sometimes knocks over the furniture in his attempt to get at the story. He delivers in a loud, clear voice while looking over his shoulder, worrying in case someone might report him to the management.'[6]

'Why do Yorkshiremen tell so many anecdotes?' Scyld Berry, the cricket correspondent of *The Sunday Telegraph*, has been known to enquire in mock mystification. In Bird's case, it springs from an essential recognition that his own life, as chaotic as it is, is better lived as comedy than tragedy. He has always possessed a deep pride in his job, but to try to suppress the manic side of his personality in order to achieve the gravitas traditionally befitting a Test umpire would have been an impossible task. Anybody who has sat opposite Dickie at dinner while he has been engulfed by laughter recognises the joviality within him. Far better to let his madness run riot, and revel in the laughter it can bring. Players seem to prefer him that way, in any case.

All good comedy feeds off a measure of exaggeration. Farce, by its very definition, is a ludicrous portrayal of improbable events, and Bird's life has always had an element of it. It is a soured mind that does not deem that to be part of his attraction and which chides him for turning himself into a 'personality'.

When that master of farce Brian Rix (a batsman for a time

in the Yorkshire Council) dropped his trousers on stage for the umpteenth time, no-one thought to ask why he never tied his belt tighter – it was only if his trousers did *not* fall down that people felt short-changed. Similarly, Bird's career has been expected to have a measure of farce. He needed no second bidding to revel in the weird and wonderful moments that have punctuated his career.

In sharing in the humour of Bird's umpiring career, it is pointless to become so pernickety as to question every minute detail. What matters is that all these stories are substantially true and, where they touch the realms of fantasy, they do so because Bird and those involved with him wanted them to do so. Perhaps that reveals a lot about the man. Often the fantasy is more comforting than the truth.

That Bird's career was going to be, shall we say, a little strange became apparent before his very first county championship match, Surrey v Yorkshire at the Oval in May 1970. Quite what a patrolling policeman made of the fretful figure about to climb into a locked ground shortly after six o'clock in the morning is hard to imagine. Security had been stepped up around county grounds as political demonstrations grew against the South African tour, which the incoming Labour government, to its eternal credit, insisted was cancelled; but Bird resembled less a committed anti-apartheid campaigner than a throwback to the days of the Ealing comedies. That he possessed the same essential innocence was undoubted:

'I drove down on Friday night and I thought, "I'll get in easy in a hotel in London somewhere," but everywhere was full because of the Rugby League cup final,' Bird recalled. 'Eventually, I got a small hotel in Swiss Cottage. I thought, "Oh no, the Oval is the other side of London," so I put my call in for 4.30 in the morning. I had a little bit of toast and coffee and off I went. I arrived at the Oval at six o'clock in the morning. The gates were locked. I couldn't get in.'[7]

In *That's Out*, Bird relates that he told the policeman that his ball had gone over the wall and he was retrieving it. Off the field, faced by authority, he presents himself in the image of a mischievous yet subservient child; on the field he is immediately transformed into a figure of authority. Quite a transformation.

Clambering over walls has become a recurring theme in Bird's anecdotage. Take a much-loved tale of a lunch invitation from his famous neighbour Geoffrey Boycott. Upon arriving at Fortress Boycott, Bird discovered that the gates were locked and that Boycott, in gamesome mood on the intercom, was refusing to let him in. There was nothing for it but to scale a 10-foot wall, swing to the ground from the branch of a tree and arrive at the front door a little breathless but none too worse for wear.

'He said, "You'd better come in now, and we'll have some lunch in a minute." I thought we would have some roast beef and Yorkshire pudding. I said, "What's this?" He said, "It's a toasted cheese sandwich, hope you enjoy it. Eat it quickly and when you go out make sure that you walk down the pathway. I don't want you walking on my lawns."'

That was not the only odd meal that Bird enjoyed with Boycott, an ex-playing colleague as a teenager for Barnsley in the Yorkshire League. During the 1987 World Cup, according to Bird, a Boycott dinner invitation in the Taj Palace Hotel in Delhi turned out to be an offer to share a bar of chocolate. Bird's dietary habits in India were extreme. On the flight out to India he met Malcolm Marshall, the West Indies fast bowler, who advised him that a regular supply of angostura bitters would keep stomach trouble at bay. Bird grabbed at the advice like a lifeline. 'I put them in everything I had to drink – tea, coffee, soft drinks, mineral water, the lot – and it was incredible what they did for me,' he said.[8] His staple diet was completed by eggs, chips, bananas and nan bread – his sole concession to Indian fare.

Bird's unintentional humour soon shone through on the field. Not long into his first season, he was umpiring at square leg during Hampshire's championship match against Lancashire at Southampton when Keith Goodwin, Lancashire's wicketkeeper, set off for an impossible second run. 'No, Goody, no, get back,' Bird shouted, so engrossed in the game that he quite forgot himself. As Goodwin failed to make his ground, and Bird raised his finger, the Hampshire fielders were convulsed with laughter. Matches involving H.D. Bird were clearly going to be unlike any other.

He has always enjoyed a rapport with the players. He spent much of the early part of the 1979 season staring at the rain pelting down over Old Trafford. The Roses match managed one hour's play and when the weather turned foul again for Lancashire's championship match against Gloucestershire a few weeks later, Bird could barely sit still with frustration. Mike Procter, Gloucestershire's South African, and rated by Bird as one of the finest all-rounders he has ever seen, managed to engage him in conversation. Soon, Dickie was telling the Gloucestershire dressing room proudly about the sprinting and road-running routines he regularly underwent to keep fit. 'You have to be fit to do all this standing about,' he said.

Procter sensed the chance for a spot of light entertainment and before long had engineered a race between Bird and Gloucestershire's opening batsman, Andy Stovold. Bird was scheduled to umpire in Gloucestershire's last championship match of the season against Northamptonshire at Bristol and was booked for a contest that was bound to provide a light-hearted end to the season.

That is where Bird's and Stovold's versions of events tend to diverge. Bird recalls a 50-yard dash that, by the time September had arrived, had doubled in length despite his protestations. He also relates that Gloucestershire insisted upon the striking of a £5 bet (the 'first bet of my life'), that Stovold allowed him three yards' start and was subsequently beaten 'by at least 20 yards to the delight of the crowd', who gave him 'a tremendous ovation'.[9] Add references to an announcement of the race over Bristol's PA system, the sight of extra spectators streaming into the County Ground after close of play and the groundsman marking out the course with flags, and an early addition to the

Bird anthology was fully fleshed out.

When Stovold, now the Gloucestershire coach, reminisced about the race shortly before the start of the 1996 county season, his recollections, although admittedly vague, were somewhat different.

'I always thought it happened in the morning,' he said. 'As far as I remember, Dickie was allowed a start based upon yards for years. He was 20 years older than me, which would have allowed him a 20-yard start. I would think that I had to complete about 40 yards while he had to do about 20. He would have been in his mid-forties at the time and I reckon he knew he was onto a good thing from the start.

'He was quicker than anybody thought he would be, but what I remember most was this little figure in umpire's get-up of white shoes and blue trousers sprinting along in front of the members' pavilion and laughing the whole way down the course. I can't remember striking a bet. Sadiq Mohammad and myself occasionally used to have modest side bets over races, especially in pre-season, but I don't think I was involved in one on that occasion.

'The Gloucestershire boys always found Dickie lots of fun. He left himself open to attack and welcomed it. It all helped him communicate with the players and that was very important to his success as an umpire. During one match at the Oval, "Proccie" spent the entire day calling out his name, just to exasperate him. He would hear these whispers "Dickie, Dickie" and swing around in a vain attempt to discover where they were coming from. On one occasion, after the completion of an over, he was walking backwards towards his position at square leg to try to discover the culprit when he collided with James Foat and fell head over heels. In the Oval bar that evening, things became quite heated as Dickie accused Foaty of being the phantom whisperer, and Foaty denied it just as strongly. He found out it was Procter in the end; it usually was.

'I also remember an end-of-season presentation "do" in Yorkshire when Dickie and another Yorkshire umpire, Jack

Van Geloven, had to collect some prizes. They were both attacked by itching powder, and walked up scratching the backs of their necks. Foaty was involved in that one.'

Even Van Geloven, normally the butt of someone else's humour, scored a notable triumph against Bird during a Headingley Test, as Terry Brindle (these days based in South Australia and among the most humorous cricket writers of any age) recalled:

'It was the usual story, it was raining at the Test and Dickie took the players off, complaining like he always did that he was getting the blame for everything. Jackie Van had just called into Headingley to see a few old friends and, when it started to rain, he went into the umpires' room for a bit of a natter. By the time I wandered in, Dickie was bemoaning his fate and wondering why everything always had to happen to him. All of a sudden, Jackie asked, "What sort of a car are you driving these days, Dickie?" Dickie told him – a yellow Peugeot or something, I can't quite remember. "I thought that was it," said Jackie. "You'd better go downstairs. They're setting fire to one outside." Dickie jumped up into the air and nearly had a heart attack. He was halfway out of the door before he came to his senses.'

Brindle, a former cricket correspondent of *The Yorkshire Post*, is a connoisseur of Bird stories, and he particularly treasures the time in 1982 when Dallas Moir, Derbyshire's giant left-arm spinner, carried the umpire from the field on successive days during a championship match against Essex at Chesterfield. *Wisden* referred drily to 'the temporary withdrawal of umpire Bird on the second afternoon, struck on the calf by a sweep'. That, realistically, is the most that the incident merited, but Bird's reputation for inadvertently getting in the way of the ball became established. In the seasons to come, his attempts to take evasive action became ever more exaggerated, often complete with a melodramatic gesturing to the batsman and placing of hands on hips. It all helped to lift the tension.

Just a week after his Chesterfield injury, Bird was standing at

Middlesbrough for Yorkshire's championship match against Northamptonshire, and in the busy public bar after the day's play, Brindle was anxious to hear the full story:

'He insisted upon rolling up his trouser leg and showing us the deep bruise on his calf. He had been to see the old Yorkshire physiotherapist, Eric Brailsford, and Eric, with his usual gusto, had given him some fairly severe manipulation. They used to call him "the rubber" and he didn't stint on the job. Dickie could hardly walk afterwards and decided he needed some more treatment from the England physio, Bernard Thomas.

'He stood in the bar at Middlesbrough and said to me over and over again, with deadly seriousness, "I should have had hot and cold foam-a-mentations, Terry. Hot and cold foam-a-mentations. Nothing else, Terry. Just hot and cold foam-a-mentations." Eventually, I managed to get a word in and asked him if the blow on his calf had been painful. "All I can say, Terry," he replied, "was that the lights went out. The next thing I knew Dallas Moir was carrying me from the field. It was such a long way down, Terry, that I was scared I'd get vertigo. I just shouted that whatever he did, he hadn't to drop me."

'As soon as he had finished the story, he wandered off down the bar to the next group. A few seconds later, the trouser leg was rolled up again and the bruise back on display. It probably went on all night.'

When Jim Love, the former Yorkshire batsman, became the Scottish Cricket Union's director of cricket, he did not have to wait long before he was reminded about the weird and wonderful occasion when Bird called two tea intervals in one day. There is barely a Scottish cricket fanatic alive who does not blame Bird to some extent for Scotland's 45-run defeat in their Benson & Hedges Cup zonal tie against Yorkshire in 1984. Only those donning tartan-coloured spectacles could seriously accuse the umpire of affecting the result, but it was one of cricket's more baffling days. In fact, the entire weekend verged upon lunacy.

Yorkshire had hired a coach for the journey north to Perth and had agreed to transport the county's troupe of regular reporters and the two umpires, Dickie Bird and John Holder, who had been officiating in their championship match against Nottinghamshire at Headingley. Sod's Law dictated that, with such a lengthy journey in prospect, the championship match stretched late into Friday evening. But it had been an exhilarating finish, Yorkshire winning by six runs with only two balls remaining, and the team was in good heart as the coach edged out of the ground.

Gradually the realisation dawned that the trip would not be a comfortable one. The coach juddered along in the slow lane at a deadly slow rate and, every time the driver was urged to put his foot down, he muttered something about his tachograph. As the tachograph (a device for measuring the speed and time of a journey) had been the brainchild of a man soon to become Lancashire chairman, Bob Bennett, it was easy to imagine that the night was all part of a deadly Roses plot. It was virtually Bird's bedtime by the time the coach reached the Yorkshire boundary and, as everyone else sunk into their seats and resigned themselves to a tortuous night, Bird's frantic checks of his watch could be seen and heard at every junction.

Shortly before two o'clock, the coach plodded into the outskirts of Perth. Morale began to brighten, but Bird remained agitated.

'Don't worry, Dickie,' a Yorkshire journalist said to him. 'We've just passed a sign: Perth, five miles. We're virtually there.'

'Perth, five miles, that's no good,' he said. 'That's no good at all. I'm staying in Inverness.' Inverness being another 80 miles further north up the A9, that sounded inconvenient under normal circumstances. After the experience of the previous seven hours, and with the friend who had arranged to meet him long having abandoned the whole thing as a bad job, it was out of the question. Whether Bird slept that night on a motel sofa, or tumbled gratefully into a proper bed, depends upon which version you believe, but he was understandably bleary-eyed when he awoke the next morning.

What Bird did not realise was that he had not received a vital document from the Test and County Cricket Board relating to the moving of the tea interval in Benson & Hedges Cup matches from 25 overs to 35 overs in the second innings. This ill-fated experiment (intended to ensure that the breaks for lunch and tea came at comparable points during each side's innings) lasted only one season, but that was long enough to haunt Bird for a lifetime. A letter had been posted to him at Headingley but, for whatever reason, had not been passed on in time. Some were quick to blame the late Joe Lister, a Yorkshire secretary not overly blessed with diplomatic talent. Whatever mischance occurred, both umpires were to find the instructions awaiting them on the doormat when they finally arrived home.

Scotland were making a reasonable fist of chasing Yorkshire's 231 for seven when, after the completion of the 25th over, the umpires called tea in the usual manner. Apart from a mild sense of bewilderment, that might have been the end of the matter. But Robin Prentice, an SCU official, intervened to inform Bird that he had been mistaken. The ground at Perth was in the middle of a park, with the nearest telephone a healthy distance away at the rear of a sports centre. Quick instructions from Lord's were out of the question.

'Most of the players thought we had gone off at the wrong time, and the Scottish officials certainly did,' Love recalled. 'Dickie was in the usual flap, although to be fair to him, we quite often have to play early-season matches without an updated copy of the rules. We had probably cottoned on to the change from the newspapers, but that hardly amounts to an official instruction. The whole thing was very vague. I don't think it cost Scotland the match, but it must have disrupted their innings.'

Bird's delightful ability to laugh at himself once all the fuss has died down is illustrated by his own description of what happened next. 'As I sat down trying to work out the best course of action,' he wrote, 'I noticed a very elderly gentleman wearing a heavy overcoat and festooned in a thick scarf picking his way towards me ... Eventually, out of breath and apparently almost ready to collapse, he reached my chair. Pushing forward his hand, he gasped: "I am 92 and I have been an umpire in the leagues for more than 50 years. I have always wanted to meet you, Mr Bird. You are the best umpire in the world."'[10]

Dickie's discovery of an unexpected ally brought a desperate plea for help. 'Yes!' he cried, leaping to his feet. 'But what should I do? What should I do?'

Such was the confusion caused by the TCCB's belated instructions that other umpires in zonal ties also took the teams off at the wrong time. But only Bird, having recognised his error, insisted upon attempting to right his wrong by taking them off for a second time, 10 overs later. It was that decision that was a measure of his eccentricity. The last word was left to an irritated Scottish PA announcer: 'Aye, they sure do like their tea, these English lads,' he said as Yorkshire trooped off the field for a second time. Scotland, becoming more disorientated with every over, ground to a halt at 186 for eight.

Even then, there was the awful prospect of the journey home to negotiate. Bird had not taken much delight in the Sunday newspapers, where he had found himself lampooned. With an ensuing conversation with the TCCB on his mind, he was still quivering about the whole affair when Phil Carrick, Yorkshire's captain, came round with a cap for a collection for the coach driver. Geoffrey Boycott, who with meticulous planning had donned an aeroplane face mask and slept through most of the journey, was across the aisle from Bird.

'Boycs is asleep, you'd better put a quid in for him, Dickie,' cajoled Carrick.

'What, for Boycott, you must be joking,' Bird exclaimed, as if on cue. 'I'd never get it back!'

John Miller, a partially-sighted MCC physio, loved to relate a similar story to while away a few minutes in the treatment

room at Lord's. Dickie had visited him for treatment for his
bad back during the Lord's Test, promising that he would see
him all right. At the end of the Test, Dickie duly went to pay
his dues, proffering a small note. 'He even asked me for
change,' Miller would exclaim, 'on the grounds that the Test
had finished in four days!'

In the late 1970s he umpired for a Leicestershire touring side
called the Swallows – a well-heeled group of solicitors,
stockbrokers, chartered accountants and the like – who
embarked upon a trip that must have been modelled on Jules
Verne's *Around The World In Eighty Days*. Jack Birkenshaw,
an old friend since their playing days together in the Yorkshire
2nd XI, went along as tour professional and drew much
amusement from Bird's antics over the perpetual currency
changes. 'If we were in Italy, he had no lire, and when we were
in India he had just run out of rupees,' Birkenshaw laughed.
'Whatever currency came out of his pocket was absolutely
useless for the country he was in. Invariably, someone would
put his hand in his pocket to pay for his drink, or his stamps.
It was a magnificent performance. He hardly spent a penny on
the trip.'

If Bird is not attracting jokes about his generosity (which
Yorkshireman doesn't?), he becomes the butt of jokes about his
sartorial elegance. It was also on Yorkshire's trip to Scotland
that David Bairstow, Yorkshire's firebrand of a captain,
questioned the history of the brown check jacket he was
wearing. Bird has never been interested in lavishing excessive
amounts of money on clothes.

'I remember you wearing that jacket 10 years ago,' accused
Bairstow.

'Oh, no,' cried Dickie, as if anxious to put the record
straight. 'I've had it far longer than that!'

Subsequently, Bird and Holder revisited Perth, although on
this occasion Holder preferred to drive. 'The journey brought
back memories of our previous escapade and encouraged
Dickie to tell a few stories,' said Holder. 'I always remember

him describing Paul Allott and Arnie Sidebottom as "Gorillas" and saying that they were two bowlers whose constant appealing made his life hell. I cried with laughter from start to finish.'

Bird can also claim to possess a unique record as the only umpire to have performed the role of a barber on the field of play. England's Test against India at Old Trafford in 1974 was in pre-helmet times and the player involved, the great Indian opening batsman Sunil Gavaskar, became increasingly perturbed by a stiff breeze.

'The breeze often blew my hair over my left eye, obstructing my vision as the bowler delivered the ball,' Gavaskar recalled.[11] 'Instead of asking for a cap I asked Dickie Bird if he had a pair of scissors with him. Dickie replied that he had a razor blade and I requested him to cut off the offending locks of hair. He was taken aback at first, but then cheerfully did the job, muttering, "What things the umpire has to do these days." Keith Fletcher, who passed by during the hair-cutting operation, remarked to Dickie that what he needed was not a pair of scissors, but a pair of shears.'

Bird possessed the knack of turning misfortune into a vehicle for humour, as anyone will testify who has heard him relate how he was robbed in the first World Cup final at Lord's in 1975. As West Indies supporters invaded the field, mistakenly assuming that the match had been won (Dennis Lillee had actually been caught off a no-ball), Bird was accidentally knocked to the ground and, by the time his head had cleared, his pockets had been emptied for souvenirs. As he was quick to relate, it was not his only mishap when overrun by the excitable West Indies supporters.

The West Indies and Australia had met in what proved to be a dress rehearsal for the final in the group stages at the Oval. The West Indies won convincingly and, in the celebrations, another of Bird's white caps went missing. Bird conjured up his own amusing sequel, telling that a few days later he was travelling on a London bus and met a West Indian conductor wearing a hat that looked just like his. Upon enquiring where the conductor had obtained the cap, he received the reply: 'It was from Dickie Bird, the Test umpire.' It sounds far-fetched, but no matter; the incident fits the common refrain that 'It Could Only Happen To Dickie'. The white cap, inadvertently or not, was by now not far short of a promotional gimmick.

Bird was also robbed in Harare, within hours of arriving in Zimbabwe in the autumn of 1992 for their three-Test series against New Zealand, although that incident left him rather more shaken and doubtless helped increase his mistrust of wandering alone through many cities in the cricketing world.

Another tale concerning Bird's white cap is supplied by Jonathan Agnew, the ex-Leicestershire and England seamer, and now the BBC's cricket correspondent. In 1986 Leicestershire began the season at Chesterfield, and on a cold and cloudy day, with the trees still not in leaf, Bird walked stiffly out to the middle with his famous cap firmly in place.

'Dickie, why on earth are you wearing that cap?' Agnew asked. 'It's still April and it's bloody freezing.'

'Ooo, Chernobyl, lad,' replied Dickie, gesturing to the skies. 'Danger of nuclear fall-out!'

Nobody could accuse him of not keeping an eye on current affairs.

David Steele – 'a bank clerk going to war,' as Clive Taylor so memorably dubbed him in *The Sun* – won great admiration for his courageous batting deeds for England in the mid-1970s. For Steele, bespectacled and silver-grey even then, Bird 'set the standards'. His favourite skirmish came during the Trent Bridge Test against the West Indies in 1976. Steele, coming in at number three after the England captain, Mike Brearley, had fallen without scoring, resisted for the rest of the day, eventually making 106. It was a tense contest and Steele had been gripping the bat so intently with his top hand that, as the day drew to a close, he began to suffer from cramp.

'By the final over, my hand had virtually seized up and I had to keep stopping the game,' he said. 'To make matters worse,

Wayne Daniel was bowling for the West Indies and had lost his rhythm and was on his way through a nine-ball over. We started the over at 6.25 and it was well nigh 6.40 by the time we had finished. Through it all, Dickie was nattering for both of us to get a move on. He didn't know who to have a go at most, me or Wayne. "Let's get off this field, let's get off this field," he kept saying. I think his bladder must have been playing up or something.'

Such was Steele's regard for Bird that he then proceeded to lavish praise on him for 'talking me through my first Test', the occasion when he was so nervous that he finished up in the Gents' toilets at Lord's and emerged onto the field several minutes too late. A check of *Wisden* reveals that the umpires were actually Tommy Spencer and Bill Alley. That is the problem with anecdotes – after a while they lose all touch with reality. But the message still held good: 'He's been marvellous for the game,' Steele said.

The first three World Cups took place in England and Bird stood in all of them. But by 1987 the tournament had gained so much in status that a rota system (which often involves prejudiced delegates haranguing each other over a table for several hours) began to evolve. India and Pakistan won the right to stage the event and a more professional outlook was adopted with the establishment of a neutral panel of umpires. Previously, World Cups in England had been controlled by English umpires. Thanks to the county circuit, English umpires could claim the advantage of being the only full-time professional umpires in the world, but cricket's old order was changing and an over-reliance upon England and English methods smacked of colonialism.

Bird's reputation, though, was unchallengeable and he was selected to travel to India along with his fellow Englishman David Shepherd. For a man who would regard a takeaway pizza as dangerously exotic, and who has the constitution of an ox, but only one in the advanced stages of mad cow disease, it was not long before he was fretting about his diet.

In worrying about food on the subcontinent, Bird is hardly alone. Rather than follow the basic medical advice of 'boil it, bake it, peel it or ignore it', and swearing by a succession of vegetarian curries, England's cricketers tend to adopt the strangest diets. During the 1996 World Cup in Asia, Alec Stewart survived for most of the tournament on tins of imported spam and was short of runs in all senses of the word.

Bird contrived to fill his departure with the usual calamities. Bassett's, the Sheffield-based company who produce liquorice allsorts, were dabbling with sponsorship of the Yorkshire club around that time and, eager to take advantage of an obvious promotional opportunity, they rolled up on the morning of his departure to hand over a large box of sweets, in full view of the Yorkshire TV cameras.

The cameras had long departed by the time Bird caught the train to King's Cross and decided to break into his emergency supplies. No sooner had he begun than a crown fell off one of his teeth. Even allowing for Dickie's tendency to arrive at his destination several hours too early, it was too late for any emergency treatment. By the time that Bird arrived in Delhi, he was in a state of panic, and some discomfort, which was not alleviated when the England team's doctor, Tony Hall, advised him to return immediately to England for treatment. Faced by the anguish of being late on parade, or his trepidation at visiting an Indian dentist, Bird decided that an Indian dentist was the lesser of two evils and, after Hall had administered a precautionary injection, it was time to bring his suffering to an end.

Bird expanded on the incident in suitably scatty manner when he appeared on the BBC chat show *Wogan* in 1988: 'I was chewing a toffee on the bus from Barnsley on the way to the World Cup and I pulled a crown out of one of my teeth. I thought, I can't go back, and arrived in India in agony. I went to see the England doctor in Delhi and said, "I must see a dentist, I'm in agony." He said, "If you must, you've got to come to my bedroom." He told me to drop my trousers and rammed a big needle in my backside and said, "Now you can go to see an Indian dentist."

'The Indian dentist told me I had a bad dentist [in England] and started drilling. The drill dropped on the floor. There he was on his hands and knees ... he sent a tiny boy on a bike with my crown to have some pieces taken out. It was an eternity before he returned and the dentist put it back in. He said, "Now, Mr Dickie, this will never come out."

'Well, I went to the West Indies' farewell reception [this was at the end of the following summer, shortly before his *Wogan* appearance]. I had a piece of chicken and out came the crown from the Indian dentist. [Shows it to the audience.] I think it is gunmetal!'

Bird concluded by telling that late in the Indian tour, in Bangalore, he had met Geoffrey Boycott, who had given him a bar of fruit and nut. The result of that, he said, was that another filling fell out and he had to pay a return visit to the Indian dentist.

As for the food: 'I just stick to the basic foods,' he told Martin Blake, of *The Melbourne Age*, last year. 'Even when I'm in England, I like plain food.' The type of man, Blake suggested, who would search high and low for a Yorkshire pudding in Karachi. Knowing his popularity, he would probably find one.

Throughout the World Cup, Bird rarely strayed from his hotel rooms, and regarded every trip from hotel to cricket ground as a potential nightmare. According to Terry Brindle, his umpiring colleague David Shepherd was worried that Bird had strayed so infrequently from his room that he was in danger of contracting sunstroke the moment that he stood out in the middle. For all his terror of the subcontinent, Bird's popularity in India was unbounded. Both Indians and Sri Lankans revel in visual comedy (street theatre occurs naturally 24 hours a day) and Bird's collection of antics made him a natural silent movie star. In a single over, Bird could convey comedy and tragedy, laughter and sorrow, with the skill of Buster Keaton.

'Dickie reckoned that before he went to India, he rang Geoff Boycott for a few tips,' said Brindle. '"What advice can you give me, Boycs?" asked Dickie. "Don't go," Boycs replied. Dickie was not very impressed. "He's not been very much help, Terry," he said. "He's not been very much help."'

As his fame grew, so the county circuit became a vehicle for his idiosyncratic good humour, and he added welcome merriment in what can be a tortuously long summer. Simon Hughes has fond memories of one incident in the NatWest Trophy second round at Uxbridge in July 1992 when Durham, who were struggling to make much headway since achieving first-class status, met his former county, Middlesex.

'The Middlesex batsmen noticed a distracting flag fluttering over the sightscreen,' Hughes recorded. 'Umpire Bird was at great pains to get it taken down, which took several minutes. When I said, "Hey, Dickie, we need all the help we can get, y'know," he shouted, deadpan, "Put the flag back oop again."'[12] Hughes' Yorkshire dialect, incidentally, not mine...

Bird has revelled in his image, even encouraged it, but he is not a calculating man. When he retells for the umpteenth time his favourite tall tales about lunching with the Queen, he is not indulging in self-publicity as much as erecting a human shield. His enthusiastic efforts to promote three published collections of stories about his career have, though, reached entertaining extremes. Arthur Bower, a long-serving Yorkshire member, and a member of Christians in Sport, still chuckles over Bird's frantic attempts to advertise his wares at a meeting of Wombwell Cricket Lovers' Society, a renowned institution of cricket talk since 1951, and based in the umpire's Barnsley heartland.

'Dickie was promoting his first book, in the late 1970s, and was beside himself with excitement,' said Bower. 'His car boot was loaded down with copies. I remember him showing his book to an ex-miner, who had been made redundant at Monk Bretton pit. Money was extremely tight in many families as the mining community declined. "Nay, I can't afford this, Dickie lad," said the miner after leafing through it with considerable interest. "No, take it, take it," said Dickie. "You can pay me weekly."'

Wombwell Cricket Lovers treasure one particular incident involving Bird at a golf and country club near Wakefield. It was a miserable winter's night and, after the meeting, Bird reversed his car onto the 18th green and got stuck. The only thing for it was for the society's chairman at the time, Arthur Walker, to pull him off with a tow-rope and there was much ado before he was finally freed. Members fondly joke that it remains the only time that Bird has ever been on a golf course in his life.

The presence of Bird and Geoffrey Boycott in the same side at Barnsley cried out for at least one appropriate anecdote. What a lark if Boycott, the most single-minded, systematic batsman of his generation, came into conflict while batting with his mercurial partner! Upon the publication of *From The Pavilion End*, Bird was able to satisfy the audience's wishes and, predictably, there was only one winner:

'I remember all too clearly being on 49 against Sheffield United at Shaw Lane, Barnsley. I turned the off-spinner safely through a gap on the legside down towards the midwicket boundary and was really looking forward to a big collection from a big-sized crowd as I set off for the easy single calling: "Come on, one," almost as a matter of course. Geoff remained firmly anchored in his crease. "Keep running, Dickie," he said as I reached his end. "Keep running all the way back to the pavilion."'[13]

Once Bird's reputation for tomfoolery had been established, it was not long before he became the victim of pranks. No other umpire in history, surely, has been subjected to so much teasing by players under his control. He has been traumatised by rubber snakes, firecrackers, burning paper shoved under his dressing room door, and much more. Yet to describe them as a string of humiliating episodes would be to fail to understand the spirit in which they were perpetrated.

Bird was not belittled or demeaned by such antics. When, on

one occasion, he found that his car at Old Trafford no longer possessed any wheels, he was the victim of a well-intentioned, inoffensive, practical joke. There was no sense of scorn or derision, just an assumption that the best and most eccentric umpire in the world was human enough to revel in a bit of slapstick humour. Every incident exclaimed: 'Ho, ho, there you are, Dickie, join the club.' As professional cricket struggled to retain the camaraderie that had sustained it for so long, Bird offered a connection with more relaxed times.

No-one took more joy out of tormenting Dickie than Allan Lamb, the Northamptonshire and England batsman. Lamb really did push smoke bombs under a locked dressing room door at Old Trafford during a Northamptonshire championship match against Lancashire in 1987; he really did plead forgiveness that same evening before Bird returned to the Old Trafford car park to find his car standing neatly on four bricks with a message reading, 'Have a good journey home, Dickie.' He really did march into Bird's bedroom in India when he was feeling ill during the 1987 World Cup, flanked by armed hotel guards whom he ordered to aim and fire to put him out of his misery; he really did drop firecrackers behind his back in the middle of a Test match against New Zealand at Trent Bridge in 1983. On the last occasion, Lamb was suitably inspired by the spot of tomfoolery – his unbeaten 137 in England's second innings set up a comprehensive 165-run victory.

Ian Botham, whose energies were expended in giving Bird a cold shower or two in his time, wrote: 'Dickie is a complete nutcase, of course, but a hugely lovable one for the simple reason that you can always have a laugh and a joke with him, as he proved by his reaction to a catalogue of classic practical jokes to which he has been subjected over the years.

'My great mate Allan Lamb was quite expert at winding him up. I'll never forget the time we placed firecrackers on Bob Willis' run-up during a Test match. When Bob's lumbering strides set them off one by one, Dickie almost had a heart attack because he was convinced he was under attack from crazed gunmen.'[14]

But the incident that best sums up the song-and-dance relationship between Bird and Lamb is the regularly-aired tale of the mobile phone. That such tomfoolery could occur in the middle of a Test match is difficult for many to believe. Certainly, Bird's conviction that sport is something to be enjoyed, and that laughter bolstered respect for him, rather than undermined it, is summed up by the whole escapade.

While batting during a Test match at Trent Bridge, Lamb suddenly informed Bird that he had 'inadvertently' left his mobile phone in his pocket. Bird was suitably flabbergasted, but agreed to keep the phone in the more cavernous pockets of his umpiring jacket until an appropriate interval. A couple of overs later, just as the bowler was about to start his run-up, Botham dialled Lamb's mobile from the dressing room, causing Bird to leap about in a state of total panic.

Regular cricket followers have been regaled with this story so often that it can sound about as fresh as Monty Python's dead parrot sketch. But, on the optimistic grounds that the old ones are the best ones, it rates another airing. Bird himself related the story in suitably hammed-up manner to Sue Lawley on Radio 4's *Desert Island Discs* on Easter Sunday, 1996:

'Lamb came out of the pavilion and he was coming towards me at square leg. I thought, what's he doing coming towards me? Have his eyes gone or have my eyes gone? ... He said, "I forgot to take my mobile phone out of my pocket. I want you to look after it and if it rings answer it." I said, "You must be joking, we're in the middle of a Test match, man." ... And the Test match is going on, and Lambie is playing away and after about six or seven overs the phone rings in my pocket ... I said, "Lambie, the phone is ringing!" He said, "Well, answer it, man." ... I pulled it out of my pocket and I said, "Hello, who's there?" "This is Ian Botham ringing from the dressing room. Tell that fellow Lamb to play a few shots or get out."'

Bird has relished the fellowship of outgoing personalities in the Lamb and Botham mould. 'Unfortunately I think the characters are going out of sport because of the big money that's involved,' he said. 'I miss Allan Lamb and Ian Botham not being in the England side. You could have a laugh, they'd take the mickey out of me. I can remember walking in from square leg once and there was some cracking and banging at my feet. They'd put some Chinese crackers where I was standing. I think the bottom line in sport is that you have to enjoy it and you have to remember that it's only a game.'[15]

There can never have been a more willing stooge – just think what Eddie Large would have achieved had fate left him with Dickie Bird rather than Sid Little. 'What can I do?' Bird once asked happily. 'They've played funny things on me throughout my career. I think that's respect, isn't it?'[16]

There are dangers, of course, in seeking this respect too obsessively, and Bird has recognised when he needs to step back and exert his authority. There must always be a sense of independence. Cricket remains one of the more socially relaxed sports, but there is no doubt that players remain in protective groups far more than they did before Bird's career began. Umpires often joke that being offered a drink is the highest praise they can get. This at least is one step above cricket journalists, some of whom become euphoric at being allowed the chance to buy one.

Mick Malone, the fast-medium bowler who toured England with the 1977 Australians, was another practical joker, and when he ran into Bird in the comparatively relaxed setting of a county match, the temptation was too much to resist, as Dennis Lillee recalled.

'Mick had brought to the ground a very lifelike rubber snake which had some property that kept it moving about a bit after you had dropped it on the ground. Not many Australians are too happy in the presence of snakes, but English people are petrified just at the thought of them. All they hear is the untrue statement that if you are bitten by one you're dead within a minute.

'So we had a bit of fun with Dickie Bird, who was one of the umpires, placing it strategically in his room a couple of times.

It must have passed out of Dickie's mind when, as twelfth man, I brought out a sweater for Ashley Mallett with the snake wrapped up in one of the sleeves. As the snake fell out "Rowdy" screamed with fright and dashed from one end of the field to the other. Dickie later confided to me: "As soon as I saw it I was trying to work out which part of the fence I could get over quickest.""[17]

Lillee could not resist re-running the joke during a Lord's Test, with the assistance of a young attendant who was taking the umpires some lunch. What happened next emphasises Bird's eagerness to play along with a joke for all he was worth.

'I removed Dickie's lunch from under the silver warmer and put the snake on the plate,' said Lillee. 'I waited outside the room and it didn't take too long for the reaction. Dickie almost ran through the door as he headed for the toilet yelling, "It's going to get me, it's going to get me." It took us some minutes to persuade him it wasn't real.'

Whenever players briefly relented, the media joined in the fun. Brian Johnston's appetite for schoolboyish pranks had contributed to his great popularity as part of the *Test Match Special* radio commentary team, and in Bird he had a willing accomplice. Discovering that Dickie was repeatedly being awoken at dawn at White Rose Cottage by the cry of a pair of peacocks which had not shared the enthusiasm of the previous owners for moving house, Johnston invited him to the commentary box to provide an impersonation. Dickie gave full-throated vent to his frustrations, along with a heartfelt rendition of 'What should I do, what should I do?'

Bird's popularity was enough for the excerpt to be repeated on Radio Four's *Pick of the Week*. The following summer, *TMS* listeners were informed that one peacock was actually a peahen and its eggs were about to hatch. It was with great relish that Johnston finally had the chance to announce that Bird was the proud father of three peachicks. As ever, Bird lapped up all the attention.

One Bird yarn that should have been taped and buried in a

time capsule for the benefit of future generations concerns his transportation of a set of stumps to an international tournament in Sharjah. He once regaled the inhabitants of the Headingley press box with this story during a stoppage for rain and would probably have been holding forth yet, his voice broadening and flattening with dramatic intent, and his face alight with mischief, had the skies not suddenly cleared and he been forced to hold a pitch inspection.

The basis of the story concerns a telephone call from Abdul Rahman Bukhatir, the prominent Arab businessman who takes much credit for the success of the Sharjah stadium, in the mid-1980s. During the course of the conversation, he informs Dickie that they need him to transport two new sets of stumps to the Asia Cup competition in which he is soon to officiate. Time is short, so Dickie frantically rings Duncan Fearnley to arrange for the stumps to be sent to his home. They arrive just as he is about to leave, so he hastily wraps them in brown paper (wrapping parcels, of course, not being one of his strong points) and he embarks upon his journey in a state of disorder.

The journey becomes an allegory of Bird's entire life as he skirts disaster at every turn. Details have been concocted over the years, but every mode of transport brings its problems: he has to stand on the bus, his parcel begins to come apart on the train, he is harassed on the tube. At the airport, sure enough, he is asked to unwrap the package for security reasons. He is consumed by worry. Despite setting off with several hours to spare, he slumps into his seat on the plane close to exhaustion.

That seems the end of Bird's problems. The businessman is delighted that he has saved the tournament's reputation by bringing the stumps, the tournament passes off peacefully, and India and Pakistan contest a memorable final. Everyone is so happy that he is asked back the following year.

'That's marvellous, Dickie,' one of his audience normally interjects around this point. 'At least next year will be easier – you won't have to take any stumps.'

'Oh yes I will,' screeches Dickie, his voice revealing his

heightened excitement. 'At the end of the final, the Indian and Pakistani supporters ran on the pitch and nicked 'em all!'

And, once again, it is underlined that life for H.D. Bird will never be straightforward.

Bird can relate a good story, but he is rarely heard to tell a joke. He can savour an episode of his own life, but he has little inclination to satirise life itself. He is a natural comic, but few would claim that he is brilliantly witty. His humour is part of him, and directly concerns him.

Take this example: he can appear successfully, if nervously, on BBC's *A Question Of Sport* so long as an artificial opportunity is arranged for him to tell a hoary story or two. But invite him to guest on *They Think It's All Over*, where the humour is wilder and more free-ranging, and he would fail to make the transition. Indeed, he would probably find it all too vulgar and disrespectful.

By the time of Pakistan's Test series in the Caribbean in April 1993, Bird's place in cricket history had been assured. The ICC had introduced a system of neutral umpires to combat the rising levels of dissent within the game, and Dickie, who celebrated his 60th birthday during the tour, was very much the senior figure. He had the respect he had always sought, but 'respect', in Bird's terminology, does not mean courtesy, deference or dread. Rather more it encapsulates admiration, indulgence and devotion. Seniority was not about to make his life any more serious. Here was a man able to age without losing his exuberance or his sense of humour. Around Dickie, people were always laughing.

By the third Test in Antigua, Bird was frazzled. Three back-to-back Tests within 21 days was a punishing schedule for players and umpires alike. The fierce Caribbean sun drained him even more. All those early-morning fitness routines he normally carried out in the bathroom of his Staincross cottage had never been more valuable. Even the intervals allowed him little respite. A metal band had taken up residence right outside the umpires' room, making rhythmic music by banging together what seemed to be a collection of old car parts: hub caps, door frames, virtually anything they could lay their hands on. Dickie was not often tempted to hum along.

Mike Selvey was covering that tour for *The Guardian* and recognised with some sympathy that Bird was nearing exhaustion. He actually left the field for a time in the final Test in Antigua because of a trapped nerve in his back. Typically, related Selvey, there was no chance of a quiet life on the field:

'By the Antigua Test, poor old Dickie had to contend with a pitch invasion from a man with a long, flowing beard, dressed in a cerise ballgown, being chased across the outfield by another man in a yellow frock coat, green trousers, a very large hat and frogmen's flippers. It was Gravy and Mayfield, the two clowns who operate in front of Chickie's Disco in the double decker stand at St John's, and Dickie didn't know what to make of it. He probably felt that it was all a bad dream.

'To make matters worse, Dickie was standing at point to the left-hander – Asif Mujtaba, the Pakistan batsman – when the ball rolled past him. Keith Arthurton picked up left-handed behind him, swivelled to throw in a flat return and hit Dickie up the backside. It clearly hurt him and, at the end of the over, he needed treatment from Dennis Waight, the West Indies physio. Dennis had to use the painkilling spray, leaving Dickie to cope with pulling down his trousers, lifting up his umpiring jacket and getting his shirt out of the way. That was three items of clothing and he only had two hands. Eventually, in his confusion, he opted to let his trousers fall and, whoops, there they were, around his ankles to reveal a pair of bright yellow undies. No cameraman managed to catch it, but if you ever wanted proof that Dickie should have been an understudy in a Brian Rix farce, this was it.'

One of the greatest oddities in Bird's career was the day that he 'retired'. Barrie Leadbeater, his umpiring colleague, was present to hear the shock announcement on the occasion of his 100th international, a limited-overs affair between England and the West Indies at Lord's in 1988. Bird was emphatic: he had had enough, and it was time for the younger breed to take over.

'I was the stand-by umpire,' said Leadbeater, 'and Nigel Plews had been chosen along with Dickie to do the match. I arrived at Lord's about 8.30, while things were still quiet, and there was Dickie already sat in the corner of the umpires' room, twirling a piece of hair around his index finger like he normally does. I've always wondered how he developed that habit. It's amazing his hair hasn't become more curly over the years.

'"How are you, Dickie?" I asked, just by way of saying hello.

'"I'm fine," he said, in the sort of mournful voice that suggested he wasn't. "I'm just thinking. I've got a lot on my mind."

'Nigel made some kind of passing comment, but Dickie repeated what he had just said. By now, I was quite intrigued to find out what was bothering him. It wasn't a clever day – dull and miserable – so I thought it might be the weather that was troubling him. It normally was.

'After about 20 minutes of twiddling his hair and looking unhappy, Dickie looked up and said, "Lads, I've something to tell you. I've umpired all around the world. I've done it all, done it all. Many people have said I'm the best umpire in the world, they all have, but I just can't do it any more. This is my 100th international today and I'll tell you lads first, you can be the first to know, I've told nobody else, that today I'm announcing my retirement from international cricket."

'Nigel and me looked at each other. We were both lost for words. Dickie carried on, increasingly frantically, "I'm the world's best, you know, the world's best, I can do no more, there's nothing left for me to do. There are a lot of young lads coming on. It's time I made room for you, gave you all a chance. I'm going to announce it today. I'll talk to someone and tell them officially. I've made up my mind."

'Suddenly something struck me. "Dickie," I said, "whatever you do, don't announce it too quickly. The weather is not too clever. If you announce your retirement too soon, and the match is washed out, you'll be stuck on 99 internationals for the rest of your life."

'Dickie looked up with a look of shock on his face. "Oh, 'eck, Ledders, I never thought of that," he said. "OK, then, you're right. I'll go on for a few more years." And sure enough, he did.'

3

The Rain Man

'Rain and bad light have followed me around all my life'
– Dickie Bird, in The Guardian, 1993

WHATEVER troubles Dickie Bird had on his mind as he drove through Headingley's Sutcliffe Gates for the 1988 Cornhill Test against the West Indies, they seemed to pale into insignificance compared to the turmoil surrounding the England side. Rarely can England have been in so much disarray. It was the ludicrous summer of four captains – Mike Gatting, John Emburey, Chris Cowdrey and Graham Gooch – as the selectors were reduced to panic and confusion in the face of low morale and overwhelming West Indian superiority.

No ground in the world caused Bird more anxiety than Headingley. Bird-baiting was a traditional pastime among a Yorkshire crowd that liked to treat him with a fond disrespect.

They never questioned his ability – in fact, in the presence of 'strangers' (i.e. anyone born outside the old county boundary) they would praise him to the hilt – but when the opportunity presented itself, that did not dissuade them from having a spot of fun at his expense. On this occasion, though, Bird must have calculated that he would umpire this Test virtually unnoticed. How wrong he was. By the end of the first day, he was besieged by journalists, officials and spectators pressing for an explanation of one of the most traumatic experiences of his career. It was the time that it 'rained upwards' at Headingley, the occasion that will forever be known as the 'blocked drains' Test.

Bird often complained that 'rain and bad light have followed me around all my life', but this time he was attacked from an unlikely direction. Only two overs into the Test, the shortcomings of the England team were forgotten as, in their place, the Yorkshire crowd vented its frustration for a summer of failure upon umpire Bird. On a perfect summer's day, he had been forced to take the players from the field because of water bubbling up from beneath the surface at the Football Stand end of the ground. It looked for all the world as if he had discovered an underground spring.

Wisden commented drily: 'Umpire Bird had always had a keen eye for dangerous elements above, but this attack from below caught him unawares. The drains had been blocked before the Test to try to retain moisture in the square. But the Yorkshire club insisted that all drains were functioning properly by the start of the match and put the cause of the trouble on the volume of overnight rain.'

The critical crowd reaction left Bird enraged. Making a beeline towards some of the fiercest barrackers – and, some suspected, ensuring that he was within range of a BBC camera and microphone – he yelled: 'I can't help it if it's a burst pipe, coming off, can ah? There's a burst pipe, there's water coming up, it's not my fault, that.'

With that, he stalked off to the dressing room, feeling as wronged as he was ever to feel in his entire career, although not before he had added the rider (perhaps with an eye upon the popular-music vote): 'It's not just wet, it's wet, wet, wet.'

England's morale had collapsed in the summer of 1988 ever since the dismissal of their captain, Mike Gatting, after the first Test at Trent Bridge. Gatting had been judged guilty of 'improper behaviour' during the Test following lurid tabloid allegations about a late-night dalliance with a barmaid. Although no-one dared take issue with Gatting's insistence that nothing untoward had taken place, he was sacked all the same. Tabloid gossip-mongering had forced the removal of a man whose captaincy and commitment to England remained widely respected, despite a recent history that had brought much controversy and no victories.

The TCCB's only persuasive defence for its action – and one that was advanced only at a much later date – was that Gatting had been replaced under the totting-up procedure; Trent Bridge had been just one lapse too many. If Gatting had made a serious miscalculation, it had been in his on-field slanging match with the Pakistani umpire Shakoor Rana in the second Test in Faisalabad the previous winter. Shakoor accused Gatting of sharp practice, namely moving a fielder at square leg while the bowler was running in, an accusation which angered the England captain into a heated finger-wagging exchange. The third day's play was lost while arguments raged and many suspected that the tour would be cancelled outright. Shakoor stood upon his honour and demanded an apology; Gatting refused unless Shakoor also agreed to apologise. As long as Javed Miandad, Pakistan's captain, stirred the waters, any attempt at compromise was doomed. Eventually, the TCCB, pressed to find a diplomatic solution by the Foreign Office, insisted to the tour manager, Peter Lush, that Gatting apologise unconditionally, which he did with a reluctant scribble on a bit of scrap paper. The England players were aghast, complaining in a unanimous statement that the TCCB's commitment to 'the wider interests of the game' had not been shared by the Pakistan board. The TCCB's hardship payment of £1,000 to every England player after the tour was a tacit admission that unwelcome sacrifices had had to be made.

The upshot of the Shakoor Rana affair was that the England team's loyalty to Gatting was strengthened. His subsequent sacking was then followed by his referral to the TCCB's disciplinary committee for his description of the affair in his autobiography, *Leading From The Front*. Gatting, understandably, was burning to tell his side of the story and his ghost writer, Angela Patmore, had sought to evade the TCCB's oppressive censorship rules by describing the Faisalabad affair in the third person. Official condemnation descended all the same. Gatting, a genuine and unpretentious man, was by now wholly disillusioned and, for a time, retired from Test cricket.

John Emburey had skippered England for the second and third Tests, but by Headingley, a quite unexpected captain had been appointed. Step forward Chris Cowdrey, who had led Kent to the top of the championship, and who was the godson of the chairman of selectors, Peter May. 'We believe that Chris' style of leadership is now what is required,' proclaimed May. The advantages were lost on one Headingley steward, who failed to recognise the new England captain on the day before the match and refused him entry to the ground.

In such a proud cricketing county, watching England was at that time done largely on sufferance (crowds dipped enough for Headingley to lose its automatic right to a Test) and, with most of the match fought out under overcast skies, further humiliation duly followed with a 10-wicket defeat.

For much of the time, though, talk had not been of where England would go from here (they changed captains again by appointing Graham Gooch), but of the mystery behind the eccentric start to the game. The story is best told through the eyes of Keith Boyce, who as head groundsman at Headingley was charged for many years with trying to domesticate the wildest square in the land. Headingley was bedevilled for many years by uneven bounce and Boyce seemed to be constantly involved in re-laying operations. In his defence, even the most reliable surface is capable of turning hostile at Headingley. With the advent of humid, overcast weather the ball can seam and swing alarmingly.

Boyce's fraught relationship with Yorkshire, who fulfil the role at Headingley of reluctant tenants, ended last summer and left him free to concentrate on the rugby league side of the operation. He retired with a good deal of bitterness towards Yorkshire and frustration about the square he had both loved and loathed. 'There's a bastard in my family, and it's sitting out there,' he once stated on the eve of a Headingley Test. Nothing summed up his emotional attachment to his job more accurately.

'Dickie's part in the whole incident was a picture,' he said. 'I still sit back sometimes and giggle about it. It must have been one of the funniest incidents in his career. It had been fine when everybody had gone to bed the night before the Test, and there were more blue skies the next morning. But what people in West Yorkshire didn't realise was that it had rained heavily for half the night. We had been up for hours trying to keep the water off. The police had knocked on my bedroom window at about one o'clock to tell me it was raining. We lived in a bungalow on the ground then, and the police were always happy to act as an early-warning system. By about 4 am it had got bad enough to call out Jon Smith, the Park Avenue groundsman, from Bradford to give us a hand. It was a terrible, wet night and everybody mucked in together. Margaret, my wife, was drying rags, doing laundry and making tea. There were four or five policemen paddling across the square doing groundsman's duties, humping water around, holding down sheets and doing laundry runs.

'As soon as day broke, I never gave the game a chance. We had had a long spell of dry weather and, by 9 am, it was glorious blue skies again, but people hadn't seen what I'd seen. I knew what had happened during the night – I'd been drenched to the skin.

'It was never fit to start on time, but Viv Richards, the West

Indies' captain, was anxious to play and Chris Cowdrey ...
well, Chris was the new England captain, wasn't he, appointed
with plenty of talk about playing the right sort of cricket. He
was hardly in the strongest position to insist that the ground
was unfit.

'Richards said, "Let's get the game under way." He was
worried about overtime – the last thing he wanted was a late
finish. So we started at ten to twelve, on a nice, warm day, and
everybody settled back. Not me, though, I was worried sick.
Curtly Ambrose had only bowled a couple of deliveries when
he began thumping his big feet into a wet area at the Football
Stand end of the ground. I was summoned on but I told them
there was nothing I could do.

'Birdy was panicking and I remember Shep [David Shepherd,
the other umpire] saying to him: "Oh, just stick three bags of
sawdust down, it'll be all right." Birdy wasn't about to take
things so calmly. I remember him shouting, "I'm an umpire, not
a plumber." They carried on for a bit, but it was hopeless. After
two overs they came off. It was two hours before they got on
again and in that time Birdy must have told hundreds of people
about the situation.'

But what about the report that Boyce, on the advice of Bob
Appleyard (a Yorkshire and England bowler in the 1950s), at
the time a committee member for Bradford, had deliberately
blocked the drains to retain moisture in the square? Was Dickie
Bird the unwitting fall-guy in a major miscalculation?

'Yes, we had blocked some drains and, in fairness, there was
probably only Bob Appleyard who knew I was doing it,' Boyce
said. 'Headingley was notorious for water running away. The
Test was later than usual that year, not until near the end of
July, and there had been a prolonged dry spell. One of the
problems of the Headingley square was that it was prone to
cracking and we were trying to keep the moisture in the square
to ensure that it didn't happen. But there was never a burst
pipe. That was just Dickie's imagination running riot. The first
thing I ever heard about a burst pipe was when Dickie shouted

it out on television. The spectators were giving him some terrible stick and he was in quite a state.

'It was also wrong to claim that the drains were still blocked on the day of the match and that Bob Appleyard and me nipped around the back to unblock them while no-one was looking. That's just a far-fetched story that got out of control. The drains had been unblocked for five or six days before the match.

'I've never seen Dickie as upset, but he was funny with it. He's a natural comedian. I think his relationship with the Headingley crowd is brilliant. They give him some stick, but they love him really, you know. He has a special place in people's hearts and he always will do. Nothing used to work him up more than rain and bad light. I remember once he was so busy fretting about a stoppage at Headingley that he walked straight into a door. Never saw it coming. He had to get some attention for his forehead from Bernie Thomas, the England physio. As soon as he had been patched up, up he got and started worrying again.'

(Boyce might also have dwelt upon the time at Headingley when he inadvertently rolled the mower starting handle into the pitch at Headingley. No prizes for guessing who was umpiring that day and who suspended play in disbelief while the offending article was removed.)

Arthur Bower, a long-standing Yorkshire member and, like Bird, a native of Barnsley, recalls Bird's tormented appearance when he retreated to the bar of Barnsley Cricket Club, in Shaw Lane, for some much-needed solace from blocked drains: 'He sat down in a corner, gibbering away about how he didn't want to go through that again. "What a time," he kept saying to himself. "I don't want to go through that again." He has always been dramatic when anything goes slightly wrong but on this occasion he was particularly het up. He just needed to go somewhere trustworthy to help get it out of his system.'

Bower supports the notion that Bird-baiting is not malevolent, but is all just part and parcel of a Yorkshire crowd's big day out. 'All Yorkshire supporters have respect for Dickie, but they all know his foibles. Over the years on Yorkshire grounds it has become common to shout at him for a bit of fun. A group of spectators were shouting "Gerronwi'it, Bird" just below where I was sitting, just having a laugh at his expense really. He didn't know where it was coming from, he was under a bit of pressure, and he wasn't very happy at all.'

Joking or not, Bird had good reason to resent the crowd reaction. They had once barracked him for a stoppage at Headingley when he was not even standing in the match. He had popped into the 1980 Test between England and the West Indies with a view to having a bat autographed by both teams on behalf of a favourite charity. Bad weather had ruined the Leeds Test for the third successive year and small pools of water lying on the square left the umpires, Bill Alley and Ken Palmer, with a routine decision to abandon the first day's play half-an-hour before the scheduled start.

Bird, unaware of the crowd's brooding mood, was strolling innocently towards the main gates when he was met by spectators trudging home in the other direction. Several of them vented their spleen, questioning his sanity and accusing him of killing the game by calling off play so soon. Dickie loved to relate that story, for here was incontrovertible proof that, through no fault of his own, the world was against him. 'I wasn't even umpiring,' came the cry.

One apocryphal story, but much loved for all that, concerns Dickie umpiring a Sunday League match in Hull. The Circle was one of the bleakest and roughest county venues imaginable, the outfield cropped with the assistance of the groundsman's goat, and the torrential rain that fell before the match made an abandonment incontestable. Not for the good citizens of Hull, however, who had arrived in their thousands for their annual treat and were not about to be denied their entertainment by a few namby-pamby players and officials. Dickie was so worried about the baying crowd – so the story goes – that, on one occasion, he retreated to the back of the stand and inspected the rugby field instead. It was times like that when he would assure all-comers that he was making an urgent appointment with his doctor to get some tablets for his heart.

Rain and bad light were the scourge of Dickie Bird. Like the character in the *Peanuts* cartoon, he seemed to be followed by his personal black cloud. He had stooped since childhood – his parents were always telling him to stand up straight – but it seemed that he was so hunched because he was carrying the weight of every rain cloud on his shoulders.

How less fraught he would have been if he could have umpired his entire career in the Toronto Skydome. He would have been excused, upon one visit, had he numbered this 56,000 air-conditioned, all-seater stadium alongside Lord's and Scarborough as his favourite cricket grounds, if only because it had a retractable glass roof to ensure that rain could never stop play.

One of umpire Barrie Leadbeater's favourite after-dinner stories concerns Bird's state of mind during that Headingley 'drains' Test. Leadbeater was stand-by umpire and entered the umpires' room to see Bird sitting forlornly in one corner with a cup of tea and a towel over his head. It had been drizzling all morning and he was bemoaning his lot: the two fastest bowlers in the world – Ambrose and Marshall – were in full cry and the more it rained on his glasses, the less he could see.

Dickie spent the rest of the interval maniacally polishing his glasses and insisting that play could not resume. 'I can't see,' he kept repeating. 'I can't umpire if I can't see.' His mind was made up. Never in his life had he been so certain about a decision as he was then. Play would be suspended. He finished sipping his tea like a man who had come to a firm conclusion.

'All this time, his head was under the towel,' continued Leadbeater. 'To kid him on, I put on my umpire's coat and told him that the rain only amounted to a few spots. When the five-minute bell went, I said, "Right, the bell's gone, Dick. I'm going out as stand-by. Will you be OK until we come back?" Quick as a flash, the towel came off. "Eh, I'm umpiring this match, not you," he said. "Gerrout of it. You can't stand in for me."'

With that, normality had been restored; H.D. Bird, shoulders hunched in defiance of the elements, walked out to face another session.

Lt.-Col. John Stephenson, in his time as secretary of the MCC, always perked up when he saw Bird frantically rushing towards him. Whatever was about to occur, it would bear no relation to the routine parts of the job. Those people who conduct their lives quietly and diligently, imagining no tumult, nor seeking any, have nothing in common with the world's most famous umpire.

'He's a lovable character,' was the assessment of the man known throughout cricket as the Colonel. 'When he comes to Lord's something always happens. The first thing he ever says to me when he comes to Lord's is, "What do you think of the weather, Sir? What do you think of the weather? It's not going to rain, is it?" Then his next question to me is, "When am I going to get my expenses?" Then I see him half-an-hour later and he says, "No, no, it's not going to rain, is it, and you won't forget my expenses, will you, Sir?" And it has gone on like that for 10 years.'[18]

Leadbeater, who possesses vast respect and admiration for his senior colleague, nevertheless relishes the funnier memories he will leave behind. He had his first proof of Bird's alarm at playing in unfit conditions when he was introduced to the first-class ranks alongside the great man at Fenner's in 1981. The first match, against Northamptonshire, passed off peacefully enough, but Lancashire's visit proved a more nervy affair. Both Cambridge University's captain, Ian Peck, and Lancashire's David Lloyd were eager to gain some early-season practice even though conditions were by no means agreeable. Bird, according to Leadbeater, was adamant that conditions were unfit and got himself into a dreadful lather about the consequences.

'Dickie kept asking me what I thought,' related Leadbeater. 'I told him that as it was my first game I was prepared to leave all judgements on weather and ground conditions to him.

Dickie was not too happy about that and soon after I had wandered upstairs in the pavilion for a cup of coffee, he followed me to tell me that he had just dropped his light meter and it had broken.

'"Don't worry, Dick, you can borrow mine," I said. "No, no," said Dickie. "I don't like doing light. You do it, I'll back you up all the way."

'Both captains were adamant that they wanted to play, and reluctantly Dickie agreed. It was a dismal day, with hardly a soul about, and as we were walking off the square, a man absent-mindedly began to walk his dog across the outfield.

'Dickie was horrified. "I think I know that face," he said. "Is he from Lord's? He'll be furious if he sees us playing in conditions like this." I said, "Don't be silly, Dick, it's just a fellow walking his dog." But Dickie suddenly veered off towards him. "What would you do?" he asked the bemused dog-walker. "They all want to play, but I don't think it is fit. What would you do?" His position having been made quite clear, we then got on with the game.'

Occasionally, it all became too much, as in the fifth Test between England and New Zealand at the Oval in 1987. By now, the basic theme should be recognisable: England struggling – even Botham's magical return to Test cricket could not achieve the win that would have squared the series – and Bird plagued by another bedraggled English summer. Rain and bad light amounted, in all, to nearly 16 hours, every minute taking another day off the umpire's life.

The *dramatis personae* consisted of umpire Bird, typecast again as the put-upon clown, with umpires David Shepherd and Barrie Leadbeater (the TV umpire) as the unfortunate straight men. On the second day, every time anyone glanced at Bird, he seemed to be staring mournfully at a light meter. The crowd was cold and peevish and the game was going nowhere. The situation was made for New Zealand's opener, John Wright, a batsman of immense character and concentration, and he ground his way under brooding skies towards the century that would protect New Zealand's 1–0 lead in the series. It was all grim stuff.

Bird's frustrations were evident before lunch. John Wright, as a left-hander, regularly required the sightscreen at the Pavilion End to be moved. Anxious to cram in as much play as possible to placate the crowd, the umpire screamed instructions at the sightscreen operators. Something seemed to be lost in translation and as Bird's impatience grew, it began to spit with rain again. The players started to leave the field, along with umpire Shepherd, at which point Dickie swung round in horror to ask them where on earth they were going.

Back in the dressing room – if one of Leadbeater's after-dinner stories is to be entirely believed – Bird informed his colleagues that the pressure must be getting to him. 'What's it coming to, Shep?' he asked. 'I'm making 'em play in rain.'

Bird has a favourite refrain whenever anybody suggests he has always been quick to leave the field at the first sign of bad weather. 'I'll stand in snow, I'll stand in snow,' he shrieks, occasionally grabbing his confidant by the jacket lapels to impress the point. There have been occasions when Bird has been as good as his word: George Ferris, Leicestershire's Antiguan fast bowler, walked off in an April snowstorm after being dismissed by Yorkshire's Paul Jarvis at Grace Road in 1985. It was unsure whether his dismissal owed most to the craft of Jarvis' outswinger or Ferris's total bewilderment as he gazed upon snowflakes for the first time in his life.

The most famous occurrence of snow stopping play in English first-class cricket surely took place during Derbyshire's championship match against Lancashire in 1975. Even allowing for the fact that the match took place in the Peak District town of Buxton, one of the more exposed first-class venues, it was all a bit extreme. It was, after all, early June at the time. There are many positive arguments to be made in favour of uncovered pitches, but this particular match was decided by the elements to a ridiculous degree. Lancashire had thrashed 477 for five on the Saturday, a record for matches played under the 100-overs restriction on first innings. After the snow, the pitch played abominably and Derbyshire were bowled out twice in three-and-a-half hours for 42 and 87.

Ashley Harvey-Walker, a Derbyshire middle-order batsman of such stately bearing that for a time he answered to the soubriquet of Lord Lucan or Colonel Chinstrap, was concerned enough to hand Bird his false teeth for safekeeping. Harvey-Walker is now grounds consultant for the Transvaal Cricket Union in Johannesburg – a post that arose out of Bird's invitation to him to do some coaching in South Africa in 1972 – and the experience is still etched upon his memory.

'It was June 2nd,' he said. 'That's one date I'll never forget. The wicket was so dangerous that I decided to take my teeth out before they were knocked out. There were five of them altogether. Dickie made a shuddering noise as he looked at them. He didn't seem too enthusiastic about taking them off me, but eventually he wrapped them in a handkerchief. It wasn't the cleanest hanky I've ever seen either. I reckon he'd wiped his nose on it once or twice.

'Major Carr, who was the Derbyshire secretary at the time, announced to us all that there was nothing wrong with the wicket. But it was a season when the bowlers' run-ups were covered so they could race in as fast as they liked. Peter Lever refused to bowl because he was afraid that he would injure someone. He had struck Ewen Chatfield on the temple in Auckland the previous winter, while playing for England against New Zealand, and he couldn't stomach the thought of going through all that again. We got caught on wet wickets about half-a-dozen times that season. The opposition would make a large score and then it would pour down. But you never thought of going off because the pitch was dangerous. Uncovered wickets were accepted for what they were. You just got on with it.'

When bad weather is the theme, there is barely any county cricketer who does not have a particular memory about Dickie Bird. Nowhere endured a bleaker start to the 1989 season than

Derby, and Bird was scheduled to spend the first week of the season there. At times like that his favourite conversation piece would involve exactly how many layers of clothing he was wearing, in what order he was wearing them, and how he could have done with a few layers more. The Sunday League match was abandoned because of rain and snow, but that did not seem to make Bird's day any easier. 'We all heard a detailed story of his three-hour journey from Barnsley to Derby, and how bad the snow had been on the motorway,' said Steve Coverdale, Northamptonshire's chief executive. 'He was in a terrible tither for so early in the season. Then he called the match off, and off he went again, out into the storm for another horrendous journey back. What a way to make a living!'

John Holder, one of the most tolerant and easy-going umpires on the first-class list, has regularly been amused by Bird's antics. He sampled his Rain Rage during a soggy Ashes Test at Edgbaston in 1989. The first day's play ended with a cloudburst and even Birmingham's Brumbrella could not prevent 10 hours' play being lost in the next two days. 'There was horrendous flooding on Thursday evening,' said Holder. 'The ground looked like a lake. When we arrived the following morning, the rain was still bucketing down, and Dickie was not happy. He kept asking me, "What are we going to do, Master? What are we going to do?"

'"We can't do anything, Dickie, just relax," I said. "It's when the rain stops that we have problems."'

All umpires have been berated for stoppages due to bad weather, but surely no umpire has ever been barracked as loudly and persistently as Bird. When he is examining a damp patch on the square, or peering upwards at scudding black clouds, his fussing around can become a source of irritation. He always claims that he is as willing to play in poor weather as any umpire, but that the risk of serious injury to players often makes it impossible. With lawyers increasingly recognising that sports injuries can be a nice little earner, it would be foolhardy to act otherwise.

Jack Sokell, secretary of Wombwell Cricket Lovers' Society, of which Bird, a member since 1958, is patron, is a proud Barnsley man who has known the umpire since his teens. Sokell echoes his feelings when he says: 'Everybody blames him for bad weather. People think he actually brings bad weather. He's not God. What on earth can he do about it?'

Bird cannot as much as look at a light meter without someone accusing him of regarding it as a style accessory. He has a mixture of approaches. Most often spotted is the theatrical stare at the light-meter reading in mid-pitch when there is a danger that play may be suspended and Bird wants the world to know that the decision will be based upon scientific evidence. But there is also the surreptitious glance at the light meter from square leg, an undertaking he almost manages without removing the offending implement from his pocket. In this case, he has the manner of a schoolboy snatching a glance at something in class in fear that it might be confiscated.

The relationship between Bird and his light meter was consummated in the Lord's Test of 1978 when he and Barrie Meyer used them for the first time. The recognition had dawned that the light meters used by cricket photographers could also have a practical purpose for umpires and ensure that decisions were consistent. Meyer explained: 'The idea has always been to leave the decision about the light in the hands of the umpires. The meter is there as a back-up, so that umpires can determine whether there has been any improvement or deterioration in the light since they took their original decision.'

When the umpire's model was introduced, it bore little resemblance to the equipment used in the average camera, but was based upon an industrial light meter. It was calibrated in simple units from one to 10 (initially as a needle and dial, but more recently digital), which made it easier to understand. But journalists' minds are naturally suspicious and some photographers suspected that the TCCB deliberately introduced a different measuring system so that the media did not know too much.

Meyer has a different way of measuring Bird's anxiety levels, something that could be termed 'the talcum-powder reading'. 'When you walk into the dressing room before an important match, if you look below Dickie's seat there is talcum powder all over the place. The bigger the match, the bigger the pile of talc. He slaps a whole load of it on his feet, around his legs, all over his body. He can become so nervous while applying the powder that when you talk to him, his answers bear absolutely no relation to the questions. Then, all of a sudden, the powdering is finished and he snaps back into life.'

There are some advantages to being the Rain Man. Over his career, Bird's presence has coincided with the breaking of droughts in both Sharjah and Zimbabwe: merely by pushing three stumps in the ground he has caused downpours that had proved immune to prayers of mullahs or the rain dances of witch doctors.

Zimbabwe's accession to full Test status in 1992 satisfied all those of us who believe that cricket is best served by an expansionist philosophy, but no-one could pretend that it was not without its problems. As Matthew Engel wrote in *The Guardian* on the eve of Zimbabwe's inaugural Test, against India in Harare: 'The moral corruption and bankruptcy of Ian Smith's regime has been replaced by economic corruption and bankruptcy under Robert Mugabe. Now Providence, moving in a very mysterious way indeed, has decided to show life really was better under white government by visiting the country with its worst-ever drought.' The considerable hardship throughout the country, as watering holes dried up, crops failed and animals died, hardly made the Zimbabwe Cricket Union's attempts to extend their base into non-white areas any easier. Although South Africa's apartheid era was only just drawing to a close, the irony was that South Africa's development along multiracial lines was much more advanced. In Zimbabwe cricket, where funds were scarce and where there was no sporting boycott to steel the mind, a certain air of exclusivity still remained. Cricket seemed as much a satisfying retreat as a catalyst for change.

It took Bird only a few hours to appreciate the harsh economic realities when he was mugged in the centre of Harare. The prospect of breaking Zimbabwe's drought filled him with rather more glee. It was a nice comic line to suggest that bringing rain was within his powers, but one sensed that he almost believed it. Why not? Everybody else did. In the unpretentious bar of the Harare Sports Club, they joked of 'killing two birds with one stone'.

'I broke the drought in Sharjah,' Bird told the locals. 'It had never rained there before I went. There were floods!' Even as he related the story, a few clouds began to amass north of the city. The first day of the match coincided with a national week of prayer for rain and Bird, appropriately, wore a wide-brimmed canonical hat out in the middle. But Zimbabwe's drought did not weaken easily and, as the sun continued to beat down, the umpire had to contend with an inaugural Test of exceptional dullness. Zimbabwe, batting for more than two days, moved doggedly to 456; India responded with 307 as Sanjay Manjrekar recorded the fourth slowest Test hundred in history, and by the time Zimbabwe reached 146 for four at the end of the final day, what limited enthusiasm there had been for Test cricket in Zimbabwe seemed to have evaporated.

While Bird endured the entire match, two Zimbabwe umpires – Ian Robinson and Kantilal Kanjee – shared responsibilities at the other end. The experiment of rotating the umpires was clearly preposterous. However much the authorities justified it on the grounds that inexperienced umpires were likely to suffer from fatigue, it prevented any chance of umpiring consistency during the match. Bird must have suspected that the umpiring world was going mad. His own magical powers, however, had not deserted him. Bird moved south to Bulawayo, where water was strictly rationed, and the ground's ability to stage a Test against New Zealand owed much to the fact that it possessed its own private bore hole. It was here, in the most pressing circumstances, that he satisfied a long-held personal ambition by breaking Frank Chester's world record of 48 Tests.

It was another immensely dull contest, destined to be a draw from an early hour, although for that the weather had to take some responsibility. The rain that had failed to arrive in Harare fell in torrents in Bulawayo and, if Bulawayo's covers seemed inadequate, they could hardly be blamed on the evidence of recent history. For once, Bird could shake his head at approaching rain clouds without the slightest risk of ill-feeling. 'Typical Yorkshire weather,' he laughed.

Reuters news agency reported on a curtailed second day's play: 'The weather was more popular than the players, some spectators cheering the rain, the first here in months.' Geoffrey Dean, in *The Cricketer*, described it as 'the first decent rain in the Matabeleland capital for two years', and suggested that the Zimbabweans were ready to believe that Bird was some kind of Rain God. Only weeks away from a catastrophe from which the country would have taken years to recover, their delight was unrestrained. Bird, who loves nothing better than a good, old-fashioned happy ending, would have been enchanted by the appearance of another ready-made anecdote.

On his return to England, Bird obliged *The Guardian* with an embellishment or two concerning Zimbabwe's worst drought this century. He told me: 'As soon as I walked off the plane in Zimbabwe a spot of rain hit me on the head. They had never seen rain like it. People were on their hands and knees shouting, "Dickie Bird has arrived, it's raining, it's raining." Everybody was celebrating, but we had terrible trouble with the run-ups.'

That cloudburst is not to be confused with the one which ended a five-year drought in Sharjah. While Bird slept peacefully in the Continental Hotel, floods caused chaos in the city. The Continental was a modern, opulent hotel, but it had never been tested against heavy rain. Sure enough, the inevitable happened.

'I'd never heard rain like it,' Bird told me. 'The next morning the water in my bedroom was six inches deep. One of the management came into my room, lifted me out of bed and carried me to safety.'

There were, no doubt, other tales, too, of rain like he had never smelt, tasted or touched. But they had to wait for another time.

One of the most renowned limited-overs matches in England owed everything to Bird's willingness to stand in near darkness. Lancashire's Gillette Cup semi-final against Gloucestershire in late July 1971 did not finish until 8.50 pm, one bout of slogging by David Hughes against the flighted off-spinners of Gloucestershire's John Mortimore finally settling the match in Lancashire's favour. Cars were passing the ground on headlights and the lights in Warwick Road station were blazing brightly when Mortimore began the 56th over with 25 runs still needed. Hughes struck Mortimore for two sixes, two fours and two twos to bring the scores level. Lancashire's captain, Jack Bond, who had agreed to bat on in poor light, must have been questioning his own sanity as he then had to face five balls from Mike Procter off his full run, but somehow he made contact with one delivery and Lancashire reached the final with 19 balls to spare.

More than an hour had been lost to rain after lunch, but the evening was warm and sunny and, at the cut-off time of half-past seven, the umpires decided to play to a conclusion. Whatever Bird's reservations might have been about completing the match, his senior partner, Arthur Jepson, had no doubts. 'You can see the moon – how far do you want to see?' Jepson famously told Hughes as the player observed that night had fallen. Jepson had no wish to book in for another night in Manchester and, with the aid of such uncluttered logic, the game obstinately reached a conclusion.

One-day cricket was still a relatively casual affair. Players were exhilarated by the large crowds which flocked to see it, but many privately regarding the shortened format of the game with contempt. In the days before helmets, the dangers of suffering serious injury were also treated much more lightly, as just an occupational hazard. It is inconceivable that a match of such importance could finish in such circumstances today. Bird equally, as his career progressed, would not have viewed it as worthwhile taking such a risk.

Alan Gibson, in *The Times*, had reservations about the umpires' decision:

'They were within their rights, but at the time it seemed an imprudent decision because once taken it could hardly be reversed. Gloucestershire, not unnaturally, bowled their overs more and more slowly. They must have been very tired at the end after more than four hours' fielding without a break and, in fact, could not sustain their effort to the end. This handicap was fully counterbalanced by the bad light, but one way and another the contest had ceased to be one of true cricketing skills. It was, to be sure, exciting, and made a memorable day for nearly 30,000 people ... but it was really no way for an important match to be settled.'

And when the skies clear, trust Dickie to be hounded instead by sun. The announcement 'Sun Stops Play at Old Trafford', where rumour has it that life membership comes with a complimentary pair of wellingtons, must rank as one of the most unexpected news flashes of all time, but Bird managed it during the fourth Cornhill Test between England and the West Indies in 1995.

Shortly before tea, play was interrupted because of the glare of the sun on a B&Q greenhouse alongside the ground. Everybody had been warned about the 'greenhouse effect', but few expected to discover proof of its existence in Manchester. The reflection of the sun was too much for England's captain, Michael Atherton, to bear and soon umpire Bird's consternation was obvious as he strode down to the sightscreen to discover the source of the problem. His antics caused much merriment among the crowd. 'Maybe it's my false teeth,

Dickie,' proposed one spectator. 'I'll take them out if you like.'

Over in the B&Q greenhouse, the thermometers showed 115°F, a small trail of shoppers made desultory purchases in stifling heat and the Muzak droned away remorselessly. As groundstaff scrambled to block out the reflection with black sheeting, and Bird called tea 15 minutes early to allow them to sort out the problem, the urge to return to the cricket was uncontrollable. Life in the B&Q greenhouse was about as dull as you can get it, but a couple of hundred yards away, Dickie Bird was again involved in a spot of impromptu theatre.

Manchester's rare bout of midsummer madness continued to haunt him as the Test was persistently interrupted by a spate of streakers, so many that Lancashire's chief executive, John Bower, called for it to become an arrestable offence. Bird had no time for streakers, although he was not so offended if they kept their underpants on; the modest streaker who merely dropped his trousers on the pitch during a Test at the Oval and then contrived to pat back a cheese roll bowled by his friend received the ultimate Bird accolade of 'good, clean fun'.

Several observers wondered whether the Old Trafford Test was the first occasion on which a Test had been stopped by sunshine. Further research discovered that not only had it happened before, but Bird had again been the unfortunate umpire. During the 1974 Test between England and Pakistan at the Oval, the players trooped off 15 minutes early after Chris Old, who was batting for England at the time, complained that he was being blinded by sunlight reflecting off the Shell building about a mile away.

When the weather intervenes, as long as there are fleeting hopes of play, Dickie Bird has taken more flak in the past 26 years than one would wish upon one's greatest enemy. Far better for him that the rain lashes down, and play is impossible. Then his trials and tribulations have been the source of much laughter. That is a tribute to his humanity.

In any case, there are always those who will look kindly on stoppages, whatever the state of play. Take Arthur Marshall's plea: 'If, as I fear, there is cricket in heaven, there will also, please God, be rain.' All Marshall has to do is to ensure that H.D. Bird is one of the umpires.

4

Flying High

'He has been simply the best umpire ever seen'
– Raymond Illingworth, England chairman
of selectors, 1996

RAYMOND Illingworth did not win as many arguments as he would have liked while chairman of selectors – 100 per cent, after all, is a challenging target – but on one proposition he would surely hold sway. Illingworth's declaration upon Dickie Bird's retirement from international cricket that 'he has been simply the best umpire ever seen' would bring resounding support from all corners of the globe. All those in favour? Motion carried overwhelmingly.

It might just be that, for all his undoubted wealth of cricketing knowledge, Illy is a teeny-weeny bit predisposed towards Yorkshiremen, but on this issue, few will accuse him of bias.

71

The conviction that Bird has known no equal is widely shared. Alongside his ability to make the correct decision more often than most, his conscientiousness, integrity and devotion have been second to none. He has a keen appreciation of what constitutes fair play, and he has an instinct for justice and the ethics of the game. For much of his career, he also held the unofficial world record for running backwards.

Bird's record of 66 Tests, 92 one-day internationals and three World Cup finals (not to mention his own calculation of 22 meetings with the Queen) is a measure of the respect in which he has been held. John Hampshire, for one, fellow umpire and Yorkshireman, doubts that it will ever be broken.

'Umpiring is a lot harsher these days,' he said. 'I doubt if anyone will ever umpire as many Tests as Dickie, or umpire them so impressively. There are many more top umpires around these days than when he first came onto the scene. It's harder now to get to the top and, once you are there, it's even harder to retain your status. There is much more chopping and changing. Far greater exposure on TV throughout the world also means that umpires don't get away with mistakes like they used to. Umpires can get as nervous on big occasions as the players. I doubt whether any decision has ever been affected by exterior pressure – you are never aware of anything apart from the players involved – but an umpire's life is much more stressful. It would take an extraordinary man to survive as long as Dickie.'

Another Test umpire, only seven months younger than Bird, was also facing up to international retirement in the summer of 1996. Nigel Plews, a former policeman working in the fraud squad, was awarded what he assumed would be his own farewell in a Texaco Trophy match against Pakistan. No-one at Lord's had announced it as such, it was just that he had also lost his place on the ICC's panel of neutral umpires and was not blind to the TCCB's enthusiasm for promoting younger men. He anticipated minimal media interest, nor did he seek any, and he certainly had no intention of breaking into tears. A cool and collected man, his was expected to be a fairly routine retirement.

Plews' progress to the Test arena was much more arduous because he had no first-class playing experience. In his case it took more than one polite letter of enquiry to the TCCB. He umpired for 20 years in local leagues in the Nottingham area and stood in a substantial number of 2nd XI matches while wary past players assessed his worth. Like Bird, he was a founder member of the ICC panel of neutral umpires and even used to favour the same type of white cap.

When video footage is assembled to pay tribute to Bird's career, one vision that often flashes across the screen is Plews putting his hands around Bird's neck as they walk out to umpire a session during the 1990 Lord's Test between England and India. When Plews is asked for an abiding memory of Dickie, that incident immediately springs to mind:

'When the five-minute bell rings at Lord's, you have to be ready to go immediately – hat and coat on, everything in place. By the time you have fought your way through the crowd and got out onto the field, it is time to start. There is no chance for any delay. On this occasion, Dickie was nowhere near ready. He wanted his final wee of three, then he had to wash his hands, and wet his hair and eventually put his cap on.

'By this time I was getting agitated. "Where are my glasses?" he asked me. "They're on your head," I said. We then ran through the usual checklist: "Spare ball?" he asked; "Yes," I said. "Match ball?" he asked; "Yes," I said. Eventually we left the umpires' room. We were three minutes late by the time we got onto the field. As we got over the boundary rope, he said to me, "I couldn't have done it without you." That's when the TV showed me with my arm around his neck, trying to calm him down. At least I think I was trying to calm him down. By that time I was a gibbering wreck.'

Along with the vast majority of Bird's colleagues, Plews retains an abiding respect for his umpiring skills, recognising that once he crosses the boundary rope, he becomes a different person: confident, decisive and well organised. It is the other side of that rope – in real life – where his umpiring colleagues speak, virtually to a man, of having to mollycoddle him through the day. Jack Birkenshaw, a team-mate at Yorkshire and Leicestershire and, for a time, a fellow Test umpire, must have one of the most succinct assessments of all. 'He was the best over 22 yards,' he said.

One of Bird's most endearing qualities has been his ability to joke with the players. He has rarely stood on ceremony, but has still won the players' respect; he has been strict, but not overbearingly so; he has ruled with total impartiality, yet is not averse to encouraging players, young and old, on either side; he has understood the spirit, not just the letter, of the law. He has been, simply, a humane and kindly man doing a demanding job to the highest of standards.

Nowhere has this approach to his job been so admired as in Australia, where ingenuous Englishmen are assumed to be a rare species. Dennis Lillee and Bird have always formed a mutual admiration society, while Merv Hughes, that most combative of fast bowlers, once responded to a ticking-off for swearing at Graeme Hick during a Test match ('What unkindness has that man done to you, Mr Hughes?') by saying: 'Dickie Bird, you're a legend!'

'I gave Dickie my Australian tour tie after the end of the 1975 Ashes series in England,' said Lillee. 'He was not only the fairest, but the best umpire I'd ever seen at that point. By the end of my career, he still had that rating. Umpires like the West Indian Douglas Sang Hue and Gary Duperouzel, from Australia, were up there with him. There are a few factors in the high rating I have for Dickie. He had played the game and understood it, and knew what went through a player's mind in certain situations. He also has an amazing love for the game and a sense of humour. I'd also say that he loved the Australian style of play. I've had Dickie over for a barbecue and beers when he's landed in Perth. He's one of the handful of umps I've ever felt close to.'

Peter Roebuck, once captain of Somerset and today a highly-respected cricket writer in both Australia and England, believes: 'Because of his manner, people could always accept Dickie's mistakes. They liked him and they saw that he couldn't be swayed. He has an essential integrity. He is a character, and he plays to it a bit, but there is no vanity or ego involved. His intention has been to serve the game and not himself. There are some umpires who seem to dominate a match. Dickie doesn't really do that. He will often draw attention to himself, but never because he needs to emphasise his authority. He doesn't fall out with the players, or extremely rarely. If an issue arises, it does not become a conflict of personalities. It is simply an issue to be settled, nothing more serious than that.

'Dickie came into the game when it was downtrodden. The game had lost much of its public appeal and had become little more than a monastery for the players. It was a very withdrawn and close-knit provincial world, but it was a world that he felt that he could trust. He was not lured by money or ego, which would be conceivable today. He chose to become an umpire because of a sense of service. Umpiring then was a poorly-paid trade or craft, far removed from the fame and celebrity status that became available as his career progressed. An umpire's life was very humble, down with the status afforded to grounds-men or scorers, whereas the club secretary or committeemen had a far grander reputation. Soon Dickie found, to his bewilderment, that he had become a public figure, that he was regarded as a character. He adjusted to his own advantage, but he didn't change in any great way.'

Such a charitable assessment of Bird's public persona largely mirrors this writer's views, but it does not gain universal approval. When reservations are expressed about the world's most famous umpire, they tend to take three forms: first, he does not give enough people out (an accusation that is dealt with substantially in a later chapter); second, stressful off-the-field decisions are invariably left to his umpiring partner; third, that he is too much of a showman.

No less a figure than John Woodcock, doyen of cricket writers, has often become impatient with Bird's idiosyncrasies, as in this report of the 1976 England v West Indies Test at Trent Bridge. *The Times* was in thundering mood:

'If possible, umpire Bird never let an over go without in some way getting in on the act. There are enough unavoidable yet galling aspects of cricket without them being parodied. The ball going out of shape is one, the light is another, moving behind the bowler's arm is a third. At Trent Bridge, even the pigeons kept getting in the way. Because of the fuss he tends to make, Bird makes minor irritants into major ones. Though much liked and widely regarded as a maker of good decisions, he has something to learn from umpire Spencer's less conspicuous manner. Like the best referees, the best umpires conduct their affairs firmly, but with what is called, these days, a low profile.'

It might be added that my childhood memory of umpire Spencer – ruminating away on his gums as if his false teeth had gone astray – is hardly complimentary. Nevertheless, Woodcock here is arguing the purist's view, and is not alone in holding it. One first-class umpire states: 'When two men and a dog are watching there are not as many antics as in front of a full house. Dickie orchestrates the big occasion to his own advantage.'

The facts do not wholly support such a conclusion. True enough, there generally are more Bird antics in big games, but that is precisely because it is in those big games that his nervousness is most pronounced. It is only natural that his behaviour should be more fidgety. In his early years he would often sprint after a lofted shot like an over-excitable spaniel to ascertain whether it had crossed the boundary rope for four or six. It was all with the best of intentions. As he says himself: 'I'm highly strung, I always have been. What am I supposed to do about it?'

The former England captain Tony Lewis has offered a more supportive view. During the 1975 Ashes Test at the Oval, he wrote that Bird made '*opéra comique* out of a serious job', but called him 'a kindly soul, cricket his love, justice his chief intent ... he acts the Lord High Commissioner with enough pomp to win him Life Membership of the Gilbert and Sullivan Society ... Some do not approve; others, like me, are happy to smile at him as long as he enjoys the confidence of the players, and that he obviously does.'[19]

The charge of excessive showmanship remains unconvincing. To some extent it is a matter of taste, and the vast majority welcome Bird's quaint, quirky ways as a dash of colour and individuality in a serious-minded age. Crucially, the players have never complained that he is demeaning the game, but welcome the light relief he can bring. Those who suspect from afar that Bird's eccentricities are to some extent artificial fail to understand the nature of the man. It is not artifice, but innocence. Friends who have known him since childhood insist that he has always behaved like this. And these quirks – so important in ensuring his widespread popularity – permeate all areas of his life. Try having a normal conversation with Dickie: he takes an age to decide where he wants to sit down, his legs and arms twitch as if he is suffering from convulsions, and then when he finally settles he gabbles away like a good 'un, repeating himself incessantly.

Especially in his later years, as we have seen, Bird has also been tormented by the elements. He makes no secret of it, claiming to kneel by the side of his bed every morning and pray that bad light and rain do not haunt him. He has been inordinately grateful at times when his fellow umpires offer to take such rulings out of his hands. Nothing has made him feel his age more than a spot of drizzle.

'If a problem arises, you need to discuss it with your fellow umpire,' said one of his colleagues, 'and there are times when Dickie would rather throw it back at you. At times like that, you've just got to get on with it.'

It might be unusual for a senior umpire to leave the onus to a junior colleague, but most of his colleagues willingly intervene. Bird, after all, has withstood the pressure for nearly three decades and that in itself is a remarkable achievement. Perhaps it should be no surprise if, after all these years, he suffers occasionally from an umpire's version of shellshock. Anyway, if he insisted upon always having the last word, in deference to his greater authority, he would attract similar misgivings for behaving as an autocrat.

Vic Marks, the former Somerset and England all-rounder, now cricket correspondent of *The Observer*, draws some parallels with Derek Randall. 'He was another much-loved and naturally funny man. Both were genuine, but both also became aware of how their image as lovable eccentrics might come in handy. Equally, they have both occasionally been known to irritate because of their behaviour. "Arkle" had a lunatic side, but he was cannier than some people realised. It was surprising how often his size 12s just happened to crunch on a length as he was crossing the pitch.'

When the confidence and respect of the players are being considered, the only question is, how many examples do you need? There is barely a famous name of the past 20 years who, at one time or another, has not paid tribute to Bird's fair-mindedness, goodwill and happy knack of getting it right. End-less reams of praise along the same lines could not be more boring, so you will just have to take it for granted.

The advent of independent umpires represented the game's final seal of approval and Bird officially launched the system at Auckland in 1993. But his own 'neutral' presence had been in demand more than a decade earlier. As far back as 1982 Pakistan's captain, Imran Khan, a powerful campaigner for neutral umpires, floated the possibility of Bird standing in all nine Tests due to be played in the country that winter – three against Australia and six against India. At that stage, the ICC (which had no formal meeting planned until the following summer) was not equipped to respond to the idea, and both series went ahead with Pakistani officials. Predictably, India's tour manager, the Maharaja of Baroda, attempted to explain away India's heavy defeat by blaming the poor quality of the umpiring. Imran's determination to promote the argument for neutral umpires became even stronger.

For Imran, now a putative politician, Bird's integrity was crucial in the forging of his reputation. Relationships between Pakistan and England had been strained for many years: Pakistan more than once opposed the umpiring appointment in England of David Constant, a protest as much about his style as his efficiency; Mike Gatting's finger-wagging row with Shakoor Rana in Faisalabad remains one of the lowest points of England's post-war Test history; and Allan Lamb's vehement ball-tampering allegations against Pakistan's great fast-bowling pair, Wasim Akram and Waqar Younis, during their 1993 tour of England caused relations to slump even further. England A's tour of Pakistan in 1995/6 began the healing process, but, as England's experience emphasised during the 1996 World Cup, suspicions and prejudices are still a long way from healing.

Bird, to his credit, emerged unscathed from such an atmosphere of suspicion. 'He is one of the best umpires ever,' Imran once said, 'not so much because of his judgement, but because of players' faith in his integrity and, I think, more important than that, in his manner. It is a very nice manner on the field. He always tries to avoid confrontation. I know one or two umpires who always try to impose their authority. Dickie Bird is much more relaxed, players respect him for that. He has made quite a few mistakes. He gave me out three times and one was very crucial – it was in the semi-final of the World Cup – but we all have faith that, if he does make mistakes, the man is trying his best.'

Bird often gives a batsman out with the broadest of grins. In part it is a product of released tension as, often after a prolonged period of cat-and-mouse, the bowler makes the kill. But it is also a simple expression of pleasure at a piece of cricketing skill. After all those years, stooping over the stumps, shuddering against the rain and panicking at every opportunity, Dickie Bird has remained in love with cricket.

'It was a pleasure to bowl with him standing there,' said Vic

Marks. 'Dickie revelled in the contest, but he would never be demeaning to the bowler, no matter how much punishment he might be taking. You felt that he was with you whether you were batting or bowling, which is a gift not to be lightly dismissed. He loved the game to an obvious degree, and you felt that because he loved it so much, all was bound to be well. He admired the great players most of all, hugely in fact. Despite all his antics, they knew he treasured both the game and their talents. That was one of his great strengths.'

Bob Taylor, the highly-respected former England wicket-keeper, valued the old ways. He retired a deeply saddened man over the collapse of the 'walking' tradition. He wrote: 'When I first came into the game, in 1961, almost every player "walked" if he knew he had hit the ball, but now such players are rarities. Now the pendulum has swung even further. To my mind, it is no coincidence that the standard of umpiring in Tests in this country has deteriorated. Men like Dickie Bird, Barrie Meyer and David Evans are still among the best, but their human fallibility is being exposed by ruthless gamesmanship. There are now so many appeals flying about that it's only natural that the best of umpires occasionally make a mistake.'[20]

Even at the height of Bird's powers, the slightest suggestion that he might be faced with a demanding match could reduce him to panic. No-one took it seriously. Little old ladies were wont to walk past, smile at his panic-stricken features and say: 'Don't worry. It's only Dickie. Isn't he lovely?'

Terry Brindle, the former cricket correspondent of *The Yorkshire Post*, illustrates this perfectly with the story of a conversation shortly before an Old Trafford Test.

'I just happened to casually mention that the ball had turned at Old Trafford in a recent championship match. Dickie's eyes were filled with dread. "Turning!" he screamed. "Turning!" He could be heard halfway round the ground and he clung onto my arm as if he never dare let go. He immediately had these awful visions of fielders clustered around the bat and endless appeals for bat/pad catches.'

Bird had a collective term for the bowlers who, he claimed, could make his life a misery: the Gorillas. Mostly fast or medium-fast bowlers, and characterised by a vocal and belligerent approach to the game, the very mention of their name would make him comically vexed. These men, among the most respected of county bowlers, would loom exaggeratedly in his imagination as hostile and cursing opponents, intent in their impatient and combative manner upon making his life a misery. By making them into fantasy figures, he was able to cope with the stress that they could cause him. He imagined them as a temporary blight on his whole existence. If the Good Lord had decreed that he must undergo such trauma, then he would do so under sufferance.

One such bowler was Paul Allott, an astute and strongly-built Lancashire seam bowler, who fell just short of a regular England place, but who commanded considerable respect on the county circuit throughout the 1980s. Off the field, Allott, now forging a media career, remains congenial company; on the field, his aggression was part of his strength. How did he react to being categorised as one of Bird's Gorillas?

'*I* was making *his* life a misery? What about him making my life a misery? To be fair, I never minded bowling at Dickie's end because he was such good fun and I enjoyed the banter. His big thing was that, if you wanted to win an lbw appeal, you had to bowl straight and close to the stumps. Anyone bowling from wide out would have 99.9 per cent of his appeals rejected. I used to say, "Come on, Dick, I'm getting close to the stumps, just where you like me to be. I can't get any closer without knocking you over. I never bowl a no-ball, Dick, so there's no need to look at my feet, you just keep an eye on the pads." He had his criteria of what constituted reasonable doubt and you had to recognise them. There was no future in hoping that he was the sort of umpire he wasn't. I used to appeal constantly, just to get my numbers up. You always hope that the law of averages will eventually work in your favour. It's all mind games.

'I'm flattered to know that I was one of Bird's Gorillas. That smacks a bit of intimidation really, doesn't it? You try to intimidate a batsman, but not an umpire. I reckon I got on well with him really. He used to say things like, "You're the straightest bowler we've got, you should be back in the Test side." I respected him as the best umpire in the country because he was as consistent as it was possible to be, fun to be with and, for all his malarkey and pratting about, you could never take him for granted or cheat him. Too wise for that was Dickie. Some people might class excessive appealing as cheating, but I didn't. I reckon that's part of the game.

'If there hadn't been so much respect for him, all that malarkey would have destroyed him. There was always a feeling, especially among the senior pros, that umpires should not grab centre stage, but they should melt into the background and let the players take the attention. There were one or two umpires about who often gave a decision that made them centre stage. It happened too often to be coincidence. That never happened with Dickie. Nothing would impinge upon his umpiring ability. His integrity and impartiality were second to none.'

Don Wilson recalls, during his time as MCC coach, gazing out of his office window at the Nursery End at Lord's one winter's day and spotting a figure out in the middle, practising his signals. 'I realised it was Dickie,' he said. 'I called the lads in and said, "Look over there, that's my old pal, Dickie Bird. He is becoming a Test umpire. He'll even practise his art, and I'm asking you to do the same. No matter how long you spend on this ground, you'll never see anything like that again."

'People who knock him don't understand the game. He hasn't a bad bone in his body. The game is desperate for character. We have become very dour. The game just ticks over. The players walk on as if it is just another game. A lot of umpires do the job and that is it. Dickie does the job well and if a player is struggling he is sympathetic and tries to help him. That's the human touch. He cares passionately about cricket

That's out! Bird makes no effort to conceal his delight at a fine piece of cricket as Ian Botham runs out his great rival, New Zealand's Richard Hadlee, during the 1978 Lord's Test. (*Patrick Eagar*)

Language gentlemen! Australia's fast bowler Merv Hughes is pressed to cut out the sledging during the 1989 Ashes tour. (*Patrick Eagar*)

Bird's ticking-off causes the West Indies' fast bowler Curtly Ambrose amusement during the 1991 Headingley Test. (*Patrick Eagar*)

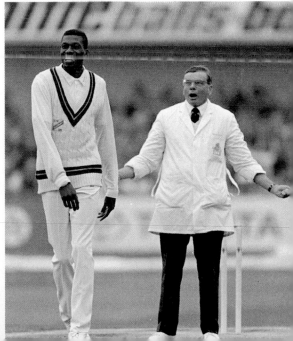

Restoring order: Umpire Bird is besieged by spectators during a pitch invasion in the Oval Test between England and the West Indies in 1976.
(*Patrick Eagar*)

Time to scarper: Bird makes a quick exit during the same match.
(*Patrick Eagar*)

'All I have to do is put on a white coat, press three stumps in the ground like this and – hey presto! – it pours down.' Cursed by rain at Old Trafford in 1985. (*Patrick Eagar*)

A rainy scene, again at Old Trafford, with umpiring colleague Barrie Meyer. England v Pakistan, 1987. (*Patrick Eagar*)

'I'm not happy, Shep.'
'Neither am I, Dickie.'
Umpires Bird and Shepherd in grim mood at the Oval Test between
England and New Zealand in 1986. (*Patrick Eagar*)

'OK, I surrender.' Bird's white hankie gets an airing during the Lord's Test between England and India in 1990. (*Patrick Eagar*)

Back on point duty, this time during the 1992 Cornhill Test between England and Pakistan at the Oval. (*Patrick Eagar*)

Treatment during England's clash with Pakistan at Old Trafford in 1987. Bird had inadvertently intercepted a throw with his shin. (*Patrick Eagar*)

West Indies' batsman Jimmy Adams comes to Bird's assistance after a tumble during the 1995 Headingley Test. (*Patrick Eagar*)

Dickie Bird can claim to have played at least one extra-cover drive during a Test match, this one coming during the Sri Lankan's visit to Lord's in 1991. (*Patrick Eagar*)

'Now, wait a minute. I'm sure there's another hat round the back somewhere.' In a tizz during a Texaco Trophy international between England and Australia at Lord's in 1993. (*Patrick Eagar*)

Dickie Bird's South Yorkshire home is a shrine to the game he loves.
(*Patrick Eagar*)

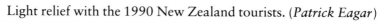

Light relief with the 1990 New Zealand tourists. (*Patrick Eagar*)

and those who play the game. And he is ever so humble. When he was on *This Is Your Life*, he never stopped crying because he was so grateful that people had turned up. But everybody felt like I did, that it was an honour to be there.'

According to Keith Boyce, groundsmen also regarded Bird as the leader of his field. 'The rules state that a pitch must be cut between 9 and 9.30 am,' Boyce said, 'and that one umpire must supervise the cutting. It's only loosely adhered to. Birdy would trust you to get on with it. He knew whether a pitch had been cut properly or not. I usually preferred to cut about six o'clock in the morning, which is a bit early even for him. There were some umpires who were so officious that they would make a big song and dance about it if I cut the pitch before they came on the scene. With them we would often cut the pitch early and then just rub a cane over it to loosen the grass to make it look as if it hadn't been done.

'Dickie is also one of the fairest markers of wickets that I know. Nothing will sway him from doing his job. I remember for the 1991 Leeds Test against the West Indies, I had to take four barrowloads of ice off the square before the match. Dickie wouldn't take that into account and give me a sympathy vote; there was no reason why he should. Some groundsmen reckon that if they give an umpire free B&B on the ground for the night, they are guaranteed a decent mark. I had a bungalow on the ground at Headingley and it was often suggested that I took it on but I never did. Those sort of considerations would never have influenced Dickie, not in a million years. He marked them as he saw them. Yorkshire was his home county, but he didn't favour us and he didn't knock us. He just did the job as he believed it should be done.'

There was a period in the early 1980s when no groundsman caused him more dread than his old mate Ron Allsopp. Nottinghamshire's fortunes had been revived by the presence of two world-class all-rounders, Richard Hadlee and Clive Rice, and Rice, an exacting captain, had no intention of contesting the championship on a succession of dreary, unresponsive pitches. The mower blades were duly raised and the wickets became so green that no-one quite knew where they were until the stumps were pushed in. On one memorable occasion, Allsopp decided he had risked the wrath of the TCCB once too often and he rebelled against Rice's insistence that he produce yet another greentop. 'What's the matter with you?' Rice snapped. 'Have you gone bloody religious?'

Allsopp, now retired as head groundsman but retained by Nottinghamshire as a consultant, has known Bird for more than 40 years, since his playing days for Yorkshire and Leicestershire. 'I've probably known him as long as anyone outside Yorkshire,' he said. 'I consider him an old and valued friend. But when he used to come to Trent Bridge, I used to think "Oh, 'eck!"

'A few years before I packed it in, we had played a championship match on an ordinary Trent Bridge wicket, not the sort to offend anybody. It was around the time that the people at Lord's were having a big campaign against counties doctoring their wickets. Dickie gave me a good mark and told me not to do anything silly in future matches. You know, these umpires are all the same. They like the easy wickets when they can just stand there and signal boundaries all day. It's when it's seaming and spitting that they don't like it.

'Dickie was due to visit Trent Bridge again for the Middlesex match late in the season – 1991 it would be – and by that time I'd been told to liven the wickets up a bit. Everyone was heartily fed up with playing on docile pitches. So we played the game on an old wicket which had already been used for this and used for that. It was tailor-made for spinners. Middlesex had the best ones in the country so they could hardly complain it was unfair. As I worked on the pitch on the first morning, I saw Dickie walking towards me. "Oh, no," I thought. "Here he comes."

'I knew I'd taken a bit of a risk, and I was ready for my holidays. It had been another long season. Much as I loved to see Dickie, I just wasn't in the mood for all his fussing over the wicket. He was appalled. He said, "Oh, Ron, you promised me you'd do nothing daft, but look what you've done." I've known him on some occasions to even tell me that it just isn't cricket. I'd had enough. I walked away, swearing and cursing.

'There was a Bassetlaw League game on the following weekend, and a wicket on the edge of the square needed its first cut, so I stalked off to do that rather than talk to Dickie. When Mike Gatting, the Middlesex captain, came up, wanting to talk about the pitch, it was obvious that we had fallen out in a big way. Gatt was laughing his head off. "Are you going to report this pitch then, Dickie?" he asked. As soon as he had been asked the question, Dickie exploded, bemoaning this and bemoaning that.

'Neither of us saw the funny side. I told him to bloody well report the wicket to his lords and masters and not to forget to get down on his knees while he did it.'

The outcome was a comprehensive defeat for Nottingham-shire. Middlesex won the toss, made 455 in their first innings and, on the last day, dismissed Nottinghamshire for 102. Emburey and Tufnell, Middlesex's spinners, shared 17 wickets in the match.

'At the end of the match our chairman, Cliff Gillott, heard we'd had a bit of a tiff and acted as peacemaker. Dickie walked over to me and we ended up in each other's arms. I think I ended up with a reasonable mark. I usually got decent marks from Dickie. He knows what the game's all about.'

It is in his beloved South Yorkshire, of course, where loyalties run deepest. Jack Sokell praises 'an honest man who has never lost the common touch, someone who has never been associated with a moment's trouble on or off the field'.

In Sokell's estimation, no honour would be too great for Bird. 'He ought to be an honorary freeman of Barnsley if they hadn't abolished the honour,' he said. 'They should restore it just for him. He could also become the first umpire to get a knighthood. The people just love him.'

Does Bird himself believe that he has been the best umpire in

the world? He insisted only a month before announcing his
international retirement that the accolade does not interest
him. 'I've never given it a thought,' he said. 'I've always said
umpiring is application, concentration, dedication and
common sense. The most important thing is gaining the respect
of the players. If I go to Perth, the first person to ring me will
be Dennis Lillee, who, of course, is the greatest fast bowler who
has ever lived. He'll say: "Come and have a beer and a
barbecue with the family." That's respect, isn't it? You can't
buy that.'[21]

There are many who do say with conviction, on his behalf,
that he has been the best in the world, and that cricket will be
much the poorer without him. What is more, the vast majority
are proud and delighted to be able to say it. That's also respect.
Just as importantly, it is kinship and affection. And money
doesn't buy that, either.

5

Eye of the Storm

'Many good umpires have found the pressures at Test level too hot. It is sport's mental equivalent of being a Battle of Britain pilot'
– Matthew Engel, editor of
Wisden Cricketers' Almanack, 1996

'You just need to have a whisper in their ear occasionally'
– Dickie Bird, 1995

DICKIE Bird has never been more distraught in his umpiring career than the day that Lord's, and the considerable might of the MCC, turned against him. The events of the Centenary Test between England and Australia in 1980 still fill him with sadness. At the time they moved him to tears. Bird has always been a great loyalist, a proud supporter of Queen and country, and an unswerving upholder of cricket's traditions. Lord's imperious and privileged ways are too overbearing for some, but Bird cannot be counted among them. Lord's exists in his mind as the great protector of a great game, a centre of fair-mindedness and calm authority. He honours its rituals with almost religious fervour.

In the winter before his international retirement, as he contemplated walking down the steps at Lord's for the last time, his eyes would often well up with tears. But it was not tears of pride that Bird experienced 16 years earlier in the Centenary Test, it was tears of anguish and bewilderment. He admitted later to being 'physically shaken and mentally disturbed by the incidents'.

The Daily Mail was just one scathing voice of many through-out the media. Its headline told of 'The Test That Lost Its Head'. More than 200 ex-Test players from England and Australia had converged upon Lord's for the great celebration, which organisers had hoped would be as successful as the scintillating centenary Test between the two countries in Melbourne in 1977. The occasion was, indeed, memorable off the field. It was impossible to walk more than a few yards without meeting a great player of yesteryear; celebratory dinners were consumed with much gusto; and the sponsors, Cornhill, even took over a London theatre for a night.

The match itself, though, was a disaster. Ten hours were lost to rain in the first three days, culminating in verbal and physical attacks on the umpires, Bird and David Constant, by infuriated MCC members. Australia then set England to score 370 at nearly a run a minute, a declaration hardly appropriate to the spirit of the occasion. England's safety-conscious reply was relished only by Geoffrey Boycott, who helped himself to his 19th Test century amid jeers and slow hand-clapping. The fact that Boycott, in the process, had moved to fourth place in the all-time Test runmakers, ahead of Sir Leonard Hutton and Sir Donald Bradman, left the crowd cold.

Torrential rain had fallen over north London on Friday night, but by six the following morning the groundstaff were confident that their night's labours had been rewarded; the square had recovered to such an extent that play could begin on time. Their calculations were then disturbed by a further hour of steady rain, but when that finally cleared, the assumption was that a start immediately after lunch would be possible. Umpires Bird and Constant, with the approval of the England captain, Ian Botham, were not as enthusiastic. The groundstaff had failed to cover an old wicket end at the edge of the square that had been used for a village knockout final the previous weekend. It was a thoughtless oversight and, as the sun shone down upon a restless capacity crowd, Bird fidgeted around the unfit areas, prodding here and pressing there. It was not long before the barracking began. The crowd's mood was not lightened by the limited number of PA announcements, especially as those that were made increasingly chided the spectators for their impatience.

As the umpires returned from their fifth pitch inspection, violence broke out among a handful of MCC members, with Bird receiving a thud on the back of the head. Peter Smith, then cricket correspondent of *The Daily Mail* and later to become a highly-regarded media liaison officer for the TCCB, reported the furore as follows:

'England's senior Test umpires, David Constant and Dickie Bird, were close to being replaced at Lord's on Saturday following the manhandling they received from a group of MCC members. Both were in such a state of shock in the dressing room after the abuse and jostling they received that they needed attention from the Australian team doctor. Bird, who is 47, was so upset at his treatment by members and by the pressure from MCC officials to get play started that he was in tears. Constant, 39, had to be treated for shock after being attacked on the Long Room steps.

'At one time things looked bad enough for fellow umpires John Langridge and Lloyd Budd to be asked to stand by.

Australian captain Greg Chappell sent in his team doctor after the unprecedented attacks on the umpires both inside and outside the Lord's pavilion.'

Chappell had been more enthusiastic about playing, but he still described the treatment of the umpires as 'disgusting'. He spoke of one man attacking Constant and yanking his tie.

Dennis Lillee supported his captain in believing a midday start should have been possible, but he has always been scathing about the behaviour of the MCC members: 'The incident was captured on television and it was the worst thing I've seen on any ground. After all the things so pompously said in the past about the behaviour of us Australians ... put under the same sorts of pressures, they proved themselves to be worse. I lost a lot of respect for them in that one ugly act.

'Dickie Bird wasn't himself ... not long after the incident I came up behind him standing outside the umpires' room, which isn't far from the visitors' dressing room at Lord's, and tried to give him a fright by shouting "Snake!" There was just no reaction and I couldn't understand – until I walked past him and all I could see was a glazed look in his eyes. Nothing was registering with him. He was in a state of shock.'[22]

Lillee's sympathies were made clear after the match when he presented Bird with his tour floppy hat, and a message which read: 'My appreciation to a great umpire, and a great fellow.' Five years earlier, he had returned home to Australia in an open-necked shirt after bestowing upon Bird his tour tie. The respect is mutual, Bird regarding him as the greatest fast bowler he has ever seen.

Considerable pressure was exerted by the authorities, among them the MCC secretary Jack Bailey, before play finally commenced at 3.45 pm. By Monday, Bailey was on the back foot, promising that investigations would be 'rigorously pursued' and 'sending to the umpires and captains of both sides their profound apologies that such an unhappy incident should have occurred at the headquarters of the game and on an occasion of such importance.'

The main scuffle had occurred when umpires and captains were entering the Long Room. Botham and Chappell intervened to protect the umpires, who needed a police escort through the Long Room when play finally resumed. Botham's respect for the MCC members collapsed from that moment, and his position hardened a year later when they damned him with silence after he was out without scoring in the second Test against Australia. Botham regarded that holier-than-thou snub as the final act that persuaded him to abandon the England captaincy. He was adamant that conditions were unplayable. 'The damage was in a crucial fielding area,' he said. 'It was not fit for my fielders or bowlers. I wasn't interested in starting.'

There were those, however, who advanced a different view, that Bird and Constant were at fault. John Woodcock, an MCC member and at the time cricket correspondent of *The Times*, accused the umpires of reducing the game of cricket to 'ridicule' and described their refusal to ensure the maximum amount of play on such an important historic occasion as 'malign'. He went on: 'Quote any law book, conceive any excuse, trump up an explanation, the fact remains that to wait until 3.45 pm on a day mostly of sunshine and wind before getting the match under-way amounted to a shocking misjudgement. Such eventually was the indignation, even of members of the MCC, that one of the umpires, Constant, and the two captains, were involved in a fracas in front of the pavilion, in which Bird, the other umpire, was reduced to a nervous wreck.

'... In their maddeningly pedantic way the umpires, with Botham's insensitive approval, worked to rule. There was no excuse for the members jostling anyone, however understandable their irritation. Equally, though, no two umpires can ever have so misunderstood the mood and needs of the moment.' Woodcock concluded his diatribe by suggesting that the umpires might go on a public relations course.

It was in a more temperate mood that Woodcock, as editor of the 1981 *Wisden*, conceded that MCC's reputation had been damaged. It took two-and-a-half months for MCC to conclude its enquiries into the affair – Bird was among those who was asked to provide evidence – whereupon the former England batsman Peter May, as MCC president, wrote to the club's 18,000 members to inform them that 'appropriate disciplinary action' had been taken and to chide them for having the poor taste to question the umpires' decision. Dissent, it seemed, was a growing problem not only on the field of play. Privately, in more than one case, Lord's officials remain critical to this day of Bird's part in the furore. 'The Centenary Test was a ghastly day,' said one anonymous but influential critic. 'The game should have started much earlier than it did. Dickie said that Constant was the senior umpire, and used that as an excuse to avoid the issue. He didn't want to know. When Jack Bailey pressed for an explanation why the umpires were not getting on with the game, Dickie just burst into tears. It was all too much for him. If things were going badly, he could be so highly strung that he became a bit of a pain in the arse. We all have an Achilles' heel and his, even though he was a very good umpire, was that he was not in control of his feelings. He was jolly good at his job, except that there were occasions off the field – and this was one of them – where he would rather take the soft option instead of the hard one.'

* * *

Dickie Bird's rise to prominence was rapid. His first first-class appointment had been on 2–5 May 1970, with Constant – a championship encounter between Nottinghamshire and Warwickshire at Trent Bridge. In his second season, he was awarded a Gillette Cup semi-final, the astounding tie between Lancashire and Gloucestershire at Old Trafford that finished in near-darkness at 8.50 pm. His Test debut was not long in coming and on 5 July 1973 he stood for the first time at his beloved Headingley for the third Test between England and New Zealand. England's pace bowlers, Chris Old, John Snow and Geoff Arnold, took 19 wickets in the match to ensure an

England victory by an innings and one run, with only Glenn Turner providing any serious resistance in New Zealand's second innings. If there was any clue to Bird's eccentricity, it was in his excessively early arrival at the ground. While his fellow umpire, Charlie Elliott, was still dragging himself out of bed, Bird was sitting at the back of Headingley's main stand, staring at the Leeds Rugby League ground and trying to settle his nerves.

Circumstance insisted that his Test career would not remain so quiet for long. Little more than a month later, Bird was appointed to stand in the second Test in a three-match series between England and the West Indies. Bird's umpiring partner was Arthur Fagg, who had played more than 400 first-class matches for Kent as a batsman between 1932 and 1957, and who had played five Tests for England shortly before the Second World War with little success, his most eye-catching moment being when he returned home early from the MCC tour of Australia in 1936/7 with rheumatic fever.

Fagg was a member of the old school, insistent upon decent and respectable standards of behaviour, on and off the field. On the first-class umpiring circuit since 1959, he had not viewed all of cricket's changes with pleasure. At Edgbaston, on the second day, faced by mounting dissent from the West Indies in the field, he finally snapped. His refusal of West Indian appeals for a catch at the wicket by Deryck Murray against Geoffrey Boycott had brought levels of dissent that he found 'offensive'. That night he stayed with Bill Ashdown, for many years another stalwart of the Kent batting order, and someone whose friendship had never been more sorely needed.

By Saturday morning, Fagg had determined that he would not continue unless Rohan Kanhai, the West Indies captain, gave him a full apology. He had warned of his intention in that morning's newspapers, exclaiming: 'If they don't accept decisions, there is no point carrying on. Why should I? I'm nearly 60 – I don't have to live with this kind of pressure. I've had to live with it for two-and-a-half hours out there. People

don't realise how bad it has become. I don't enjoy umpiring
Tests any more. There is so much at stake ... the game has
changed, and not for the better. Umpires are under terrific
pressure.'

Bird, a junior umpire caught up in a gathering crisis, viewed
the whole situation with unconcealed dismay. His insistence
that he appealed to Fagg to stop worrying cannot be read in the
light of his own career without a measure of amusement.

Boycott's recollection was particularly supportive of Fagg's
action:

'Early in the innings, the West Indies appealed for a catch
behind off Keith Boyce. Arthur Fagg turned it down and there
followed the worst conduct I can remember from a Test team
on English soil. Rohan Kanhai was the captain and the
ringleader, pouring out a steady stream of invective against me,
Fagg and anything faintly non-Caribbean ... I admired Fagg's
strength of character. The situation was unbelievably tense and
strained on the field ... The West Indies made little attempt to
conceal their contempt for the umpire ... The West Indies'
demeanour and many of their remarks were a disgrace. It is
probably ironic, and certainly sad, but if I had to recall my first
encounter with pure racism on a cricket field, it would be from
the West Indies team at Edgbaston in 1973.'[23]

Before play was set to resume on Saturday, a stand-off
between the offended parties took place in the Edgbaston
pavilion. Kanhai was willing to state officially that he was happy
with Fagg's umpiring, but he refused to apologise. Raymond
Illingworth, England's captain and (as John Woodcock shrewdly
reminded his readers in *The Times*) 'no great apologist himself',
tried to persuade Kanhai that an apology would settle the
matter, but found him unyielding.

Eventually, both teams took the field without Fagg, with Alan
Oakman, the Warwickshire coach, standing in as an emergency
umpire. Alec Bedser, the chairman of selectors, spent frantic
moments trying to persuade Fagg to relent. After one over, the
umpire took the field to sympathetic applause – the affair having

been widely publicised in that morning's newspapers. He looked rather a sad and isolated figure – certainly his protest had been unorthodox to say the least – but he had made his stand in single-minded fashion. If cricket's authorities had hitherto managed to ignore the evidence of mounting dissent at international level, they could do so no longer.

Peter Laker, in *The Daily Mirror*, accused Fagg of indulging in 'Jungle Law' by putting his own feelings before the needs of his profession. He went on: 'Predictably, the sequel was an abrasive morning's play in which Kanhai and company dragged the over rate down to an unforgivable 13 overs an hour. The session was further marred by a string of bouncers from Bernard Julian and Keith Boyce.'

England scored only 40 runs in the session, with Boycott, determined that his concentration would not be broken, leaving the field to catcalls; he might have thought that the special circumstances of the morning's play were worthy of more sympathy. Laker then reported that 'the next bizarre incident of this nonsensical match' was a lunchtime lecture from Fagg and Bird on the appalling over rate. It had the desired effect.

It seems relevant to wonder what effect this incident had on an inexperienced and impressionable junior umpire. It is not too fanciful to suggest that Bird's determination to foster happy relations between players and officials might have been strengthened to some extent by the ill-tempered atmosphere at Edgbaston. The umpire's word would always remain law, but that did not mean that it would always be accepted without resentment. A greater understanding – a bond even – between players and umpires was necessary. The master and pupil relationship could no longer automatically assure an umpire of a position of unchallenged authority. Certainly the advice given by James Lillywhite, in 1866, to a fielding side bore little resemblance to the high-pressure appealing which Bird had already realised was the very stuff of the modern game: 'Do not ask the umpire unless you think the batsman is out,' Lillywhite advised. 'It is not cricket to keep asking the umpire questions.'

As his career progressed, Bird began to appreciate that it was to his advantage to introduce his own more personalised style at Test level. If players' behaviour was not always held in check by a recognition of the umpire's authority, perhaps it could be tempered by a personal rapport with the individual umpire concerned. If that umpire was recognised as both impartial and entertaining then the bond might prove to be strong.

The breakdown in understanding between Fagg and the West Indies team was in part a collapse of trust, made worse by clashes of culture and different generations. Years later, when Mike Gatting and the Pakistani umpire Shakoor Rana fell out in Faisalabad, different cultures were conflicting just as disastrously. The next generation had failed to learn from the mistakes of its predecessors. Dickie Bird has consistently crossed that cultural divide, the number of occasions when visiting Test sides requested his appointment as one of the umpires underlining that he was as highly regarded outside England as within it. That has required a remarkable gift.

Only a fortnight passed before Bird umpired in the third and final Test of that 1973 series – barely time for him to repair frayed nerves! – and, once again, if he became the centre of attention, he could not be held accountable. England v West Indies at Lord's, over August Bank Holiday, became known as the bomb-scare Test. Some 57 years after the Easter Uprising in Dublin, Britain was experiencing a fresh wave of IRA terrorism. The Conservative government led by Edward Heath was holding emergency consultations over whether the IRA should be made an illegal organisation. British soldiers returning from leave after the Bank Holiday were advised to travel in civilian clothes to reduce the possibility of attack. A secretary at the House of Commons was injured when a letter bomb exploded in her face. It was a time of bomb outrages throughout Britain. The nation gritted its teeth and plodded on as if nothing untoward was happening, but in London, especially, there was a sense of nerve-racking uncertainty.

The West Indies, it should be remarked, never at any time

suggested that the tour might have to be abandoned. English sporting events have never been affected by terrorism (it would require an uncompromisingly right-wing view to regard the successful anti-apartheid protests against the 1970 South Africa tour in such a light). Sri Lanka, for one, might look upon such loyalty to England, consider the alacrity with which New Zealand, Australia and the West Indies have pulled out of matches in Colombo in the past decade because of terrorist activity by the LTTE, and regard themselves as distinctly unfortunate.

At Lord's, before a big Bank Holiday Saturday crowd, England were forced to follow on against a West Indies side which was coming to the end of its lean years, so much so that they were to thrash England by an innings and 226 runs to take the series 2–0. *The Times* saw fit to opine: 'Lord's rout presages end of Illingworth era.' John Woodcock's assertion in *The Times* concerning 'a drabness about England's cricket at the moment, a lack of lustre and ingenuity,' was made in 1973, but it could easily have referred to their World Cup performances 23 years later.

In fact, the similarities were striking. As the 1996 season was about to begin, and Bird by now contemplated his final Test, another Illingworth era was drawing to a close, this time his chairmanship of selectors; and IRA bombs were once again causing havoc in central London.

A bomb scare in mid-afternoon of the 1973 match caused 85 minutes to be lost, and the half-hour overtime added at the end of the day produced the collector's item of Geoffrey Boycott out hooking twice in the same match. Boycott's mood was not enhanced when he was molested as he left the field. He had surrendered his wicket in the last over of the day through hot-headedness, angry that Brian Luckhurst (who preferred to remain at the non-striker's end) had just refused an easy single. The spectators who jostled him were fortunate merely to be met with a bit of choice Anglo-Saxon, rather than the meat of a scything Slazenger.

One consequence of that crowd behaviour was that spectators were banned from the grass beyond the boundary rope at future matches at Lord's. With every passing month, cricket was having to give more serious consideration to its control of the game on and off the field. When the bomb hoax stopped the game the MCC secretary, Billy Griffith, advised the 28,000 spectators to leave the ground, primarily for their own safety, but also to assist the police in their efforts to search the ground. A few left, but many stayed in their seats – remarking, no doubt, that they were not about to be swayed by IRA terrorism – while a thousand or more swarmed towards the square, logically calculating that it was the safest place in the ground. Cricket, as John Arlott remarked in *The Guardian*, was 'pathetically vulnerable to the bomb threat'. The freedom to leave unattended bags for hours anywhere in a cricket ground and wander back in due course to find them untampered with was part of the very fabric of the game. Such behaviour suited the cricket watcher's disposition and, indeed, still does. It provided further proof that a cricket ground was, indeed, a place of seclusion which might be a million miles removed from an increasingly hectic and lawless world.

One memory of that occasion has proved more durable than the rest. It was the photograph of Dickie Bird perched on the covers, happily nattering away to hundreds of spectators. Black and white faces, many of them young, are gazing on as if amused by his every word. One spectator is formally dressed in shirt and tie, another is bare-chested.

That summer's series against the West Indies had been blighted: by rising dissent on the field, by growing unruliness among spectators and, finally, by the threat of terrorism. Cricket, also having to come to terms with the increasing popularity of the one-day game, and the demands of players for greater financial reward, was stricken with uncertainty. And, in the middle of the crisis, an ingenuous South Yorkshire umpire was keeping people's spirits up. Bird, unwittingly, had become a symbol of sport's underlying optimism. However demanding the circumstances, his expression reminded us that sport was meant to be fun and, with the right approach, had the capacity to remain so, whatever the pressures. He did not sit on the covers because it would draw attention to himself. He was out there because he, like many of those around him, had decided that there was no safer place to be. And, anyway, he was also determined to protect his beloved Test pitch. Otherwise, the match might have to be abandoned. And that really would have been a disaster. Eventually, the police requested that the players of both teams and the umpires leave the field, and they took refuge in a hospitality tent behind the pavilion. But the point had been made; Bird was the central figure in one of the year's most memorable pictures.

*   *   *

Cricket's administrators had finally begun to recognise, with some reluctance, that it was futile to resist the public's appetite for the one-day game. The first World Cup, played in England in 1975, quickened the move towards a more volatile and highly pressurised form of international cricket. The tournament finished in chaos as the closing moments of the final between the West Indies and Australia were interrupted by a pitch invasion. Bird had never experienced such commotion and realised from that moment that international umpiring was never going to be the same again.

Although many felt uncomfortable with the way the game was heading – Brian Close, when Yorkshire captain, had suggested upon the introduction of the 40-over Sunday League in 1969 that the players should put on silly hats and red noses – the first World Cup had immediate appeal to a wider audience. With the growing attraction of TV coverage – by now colour TV sets were widespread – cricket moved further away from the recessionary years of the 1960s. Many younger spectators, or those with only a casual interest, preferred the instant attractions of a match settled in one day, rather than submitting themselves to the longeurs of a five-day Test.

Demands for instant satisfaction were seen in all areas of life – food, music, sex – and cricket was not about to escape the trend.

The event was small beer compared to the chaotic and commercially-orientated tournament in India in 1996. Only 158,000 people watched the 15 games in 1975 – a figure matched in India by the two semi-finals in Calcutta and Chandigarh alone. For Bird, though, the timing could not have been better. Five years into his first-class umpiring career, and with his Test career already attracting attention, he had established himself as one of the best officials in the game, and his appeal as a character was much in tune with the marketing men's wishes. Spectators could readily identify with the gibbering and twitching Yorkshireman in his trademark white cap.

The final between the West Indies and Australia lived up to all expectations. The West Indies, after slipping initially to 50 for three, recovered to 291 for eight, a commanding if not invincible total. They were driven there by an outstanding century by Clive Lloyd, whose eventual dismissal tested umpire Bird's nerve. Bird was confident that Lloyd had edged Australia's left-arm swing bowler Gary Gilmour down the legside, but he needed to confirm with his partner at square leg, Tommy Spencer, to ascertain whether the ball had carried to wicketkeeper Rodney Marsh.

It is a feature of Lord's that a slight dip can occasionally make catches difficult to spot when umpiring from the Nursery End and Lloyd, with perfect justification, stood his ground. Spencer assured Bird that the ball had carried, and Dickie's mind was set at rest that evening when he dared to watch the TV replay. Even then, some commentators – the veteran Australian Jack Fingleton among them – took exception to what they regarded as Bird's theatrical tendency as he strode slowly back from square leg to behind the stumps, whereupon he raised his finger with a flourish. Bird, though, was merely intent on getting the decision right and then delivering it with the utmost correctness. In later years, confident of his stature, he might have settled for a nod at Lloyd from square leg. But those who suggested that, had Lloyd been on 99 and not 102, Bird's behaviour could have aggravated the West Indies supporters were guilty of manufacturing a worthless debate.

The occasion drew a vintage piece of commentary on BBC Radio from John Arlott. When Lloyd reached his hundred, Arlott observed: 'Dickie Bird is having a wonderful time signalling everything, including "Stop" to the traffic coming on from behind.'

Bird's judgement in giving Lloyd out was not his only impressive decision that day. Early in the West Indies innings, their left-handed opener Roy Fredericks had hooked a not very short delivery from Lillee over fine leg for six, a feat that left the Australian fast bowler applauding in mid-pitch. It was then that Bird informed him that Fredericks was out, having trod on his wicket in executing the shot and dislodged his leg bail.

Australia batted confidently in reply before a succession of run-outs left them in disarray. Viv Richards twice threw down the stumps from side on to remove Alan Turner and Greg Chappell, and it was also Richards' retrieval that allowed Lloyd to run out Ian Chappell for 62. He had disappointed with the bat, making only five, but had made an outstanding contribution in the field. When Australia's last man, Jeff Thomson, joined Dennis Lillee, they were 233 for nine and defeat looked imminent. The West Indies supporters were unable to suppress their excitement and when Lillee drove Vanburn Holder to Alvin Kallicharran at cover, hundreds of spectators swarmed onto the field. Bird was dazed by an accidental bash on the head. When he finally recovered his poise, he realised that not everything was as it should be. A sweater belonging to the Australian fast bowler Jeff Thomson, his spare bails and ball, and his white cap had been pinched.

Amid the celebrations, nobody had noticed that umpire Spencer had ruled Holder's delivery a no-ball; Kallicharran had shied at the stumps and missed, and as the crowd advanced, Thomson and Lillee had started running. Certainly umpire

Bird, with reason to feel groggy, could not have provided a perfect description.

'We ran a fair few runs,' recalled Thomson later, 'but the umpire was only going to give us two. I said, "Hey, how much are you going to give us for that?" and Tom Spencer says, "Two" – real abrupt. "Pig's arse!" I shouted. "We've been running up and down here all afternoon. Who are you kidding?"'

Bird intervened and the resulting discussions ensured that Australia gained four runs, on the grounds that the ball had been stopped on its way to the boundary by a spectator. Once order had been restored, the match resumed, with Lillee and Thomson extending their last-wicket stand to 41 before Thomson was run out by the wicketkeeper, Deryck Murray, with 18 runs still needed from eight deliveries. The West Indies had won an inaugural World Cup that had already gained its place in the cricketing calendar. As they picked their way towards the dressing rooms through another invasion, Lillee joked to Bird that he and Thomson had actually run 17 – he was not far wrong.

Bird's day had been an arduous one. He had arrived at the ground at 8.30 that morning and did not complete the after-match awards ceremony until nearly 9 pm, but he was not complaining. 'It was the greatest game of cricket I had ever seen,' he said. 'I felt privileged to have played a part in it.'[24] The Australians were impressed too, and their manager, Fred Bennett, dropped Bird a note in praise of his efforts in the most trying circumstances.

There was still occasion to cram in a four-Test Ashes series after the World Cup, a series that Australia won 1–0 thanks to two England batting collapses at Edgbaston, where Bird's own efficiency was undermined by a bad back which forced him temporarily to give way to Alan Oakman, Warwickshire's coach, at tea on the third day. The recognisable Bird stoop was achieved a little more gingerly for the rest of the summer.

At the Oval, the final Test of the series, he became involved in several run-ins with Dennis Lillee which in fact launched their enduring friendship. An argument in the middle of an over about whether the ball was out of shape reached such an impasse that everybody sat down. Eventually Lillee completed the over by way of protest by bowling three off-spinners. Lillee recalled the incident as follows: 'At one stage I was trying to bowl fast with something that looked as though it had been through a mincer. I approached umpire Dickie Bird and asked him if he would change the ball. He examined it and replied that I should keep on bowling with it. I said, "I'm not going to bowl with that thing. No batsman has to bat with an inferior bat. It's out of shape and split and I'd like it changed."'[25]

There followed a digging in of heels on both sides, at which point Bird told Ian Chappell, the Australian captain, that he would examine the ball at the end of the over. Lillee recalled: 'Ian looked at me and said, "You'd better complete the over, pal." I said I would, but only bowling off-spinners. At the end of the over Dickie said they were some of the best offies he'd ever seen. Trust Dickie to put the matter to rest in such a manner ... He really is a very funny man, apart from being one of the best umpires I've seen in my career ... It's a great thing for players to feel they can relate to an umpire as a human being – though not to the extent of overdoing it. I'm sure Dickie would be the first to pull the reins – if he felt he had to. But his attitude certainly makes you feel more at ease with umpires' decisions.'[26]

* * *

Perhaps the most disturbing sight for an umpire is when a fast bowler delivers a beamer. Dissent, gamesmanship and a stream of bouncers all pale into insignificance when compared to the head-high full toss aimed straight at the batsman. It is a potentially life-threatening delivery, much more dangerous than the bouncer: totally unexpected, much more difficult to see and desperately hard to avoid. It is a delivery that courts such controversy that it invariably attracts a media storm, although it is a courageous – or foolhardy – journalist who claims that a beamer was bowled deliberately. Nevertheless, one tabloid cricket writer's enthusiasm for 'beamer' stories is such that it has led him to be nicknamed 'Killer Ball'.

Bird's first experience of the beamer as an umpire came during Pakistan's Test at the Oval in 1974. It was bowled by Sarfraz Nawaz at the England captain, Tony Greig. As the ball flew past his head (quite an achievement, for Greig was 6ft 6in tall), Bird flapped so much that, had there been a fresh breeze, he might easily have flown out of the ground. But he regained his composure with alacrity as the two players squared up to each other.

Most umpires, if asked to describe the incident, would adopt a grave and dignified expression and explain that it was really something of a storm in a teacup, all dealt with quite satisfactorily in a couple of seconds. Not Dickie. He relived the incident with his usual gusto in a guest appearance on *Wogan* on BBC TV in 1988:

'In came Sarfraz and bowled a beamer at Greigy which whistled like a tracer bullet past his chin and into the wicketkeeper's gloves. It knocked him onto his backside, that's how quick it was. Greig walked down the pitch and said, "You so-and-so, I'm going to knock your head off with this bat," and Sarfraz said, "You South African so-and-so, I am waiting for you." And both of them came for each other and I thought, "What do I do now?" and I shouted, "Gentlemen, that's tea," picked the bails off, and off we walked.' Rarely can a tea interval have come along so conveniently.

Bird's reduction of potentially destructive incidents into music-hall comedy is not only part of his charm, but part of his singular gift as an umpire. Maintaining a sober pretence that the matter has been properly dealt with would immediately make an issue of it. Bird's way was to control the immediate situation, and then laugh it all off, invoking the essential camaraderie of the game. While other umpires were struggling to combat rising levels of dissent in the game, Bird's individual style was keeping controversy in check. Such an approach became increasingly difficult in the later years of his career. Bird might still have quelled the situation, but that would not have been the end of the matter. Undoubtedly, Sarfraz and Greig would have been fined, or even suspended, by today's ICC match referee.

Greig's belligerence irritated bowlers throughout his career, but further investigations revealed that on this occasion he was entirely blameless. Sarfraz later suggested that his anger had been aimed at the other England batsman, Keith Fletcher, who had been persistently interrupting play because of movement behind the bowler's arm; Sarfraz was so aggravated that he had not realised the batsmen had crossed for a single. The only problem with Sarfraz – then as now – was that it was difficult to discern whether he was being serious.

Greig complained two years later about the disturbing number of beamers bowled during England's 1976 Test series against the West Indies. Clive Lloyd, the West Indies' captain, was vexed by suggestions that some of them might have been deliberate. But there was no doubt that Greig had provoked the opposition. Here was the England captain, after all, who had announced that he intended to make the West Indies 'grovel'. He was just talking up England's chances, but it was still about as senseless a remark as can ever have been made by an England captain in the history of the game, especially by one speaking with a South African accent.

At Lord's, Bird was the square leg umpire when a beamer from Michael Holding flew past Greig's head. 'I just closed my eyes and ducked,' Greig said at that evening's press conference. 'We have had a few of those deliveries bowled by the West Indies so far and I hope for the game's sake that it doesn't degenerate into a situation where beamers become acceptable. Anyone can bowl beamers. Now and again they can happen by mistake but the situation can arise when people start retaliating.'

The ICC, nevertheless, was sufficiently concerned to re-emphasise that beamers were illegal.

* * *

Few English summers have captured the cricket lover's imagination like that of 1981. It was an Ashes series which held the nation in thrall as England, inspired by Ian Botham and Bob Willis, stormed to two extraordinary Test victories against Australia in little more than a fortnight. Both matches, at Headingley and then at Edgbaston, stretched credulity to the limit as England recovered to win from seemingly impossible positions. Cricket had not attracted such widespread attention for years, and the royal wedding of Prince Charles and Lady Diana Spencer added to the country's animated and patriotic mood.

England's 18-run win at Headingley, after following on, coincided with the return as captain of Mike Brearley. Botham, freed from a responsibility that had weighed heavily upon him, changed the game's course by thrashing an uninhibited 149 not out. As an attacking innings in defiance of seemingly insurmountable odds it has had few equals. Even then, with only 130 needed, Australia were confident of victory, only for Willis to roar down the hill like a man possessed, his eight for 43 representing the best figures of his career.

Bird stood in the fourth Test at Edgbaston, with nobody expecting to witness such scenes again. It was a tense, low-scoring match, and when Australia required only 151 for victory, the assumption was that miracles did not happen twice. But the psychological damage done to Australia's batting at Headingley proved to be vast. From 87 for three, they collapsed to 121 all out, with Botham conjuring a spell of five for one that owed as much to the sheer force of his personality as the skill of his bowling.

Willis, still fired up after his exploits at Headingley, provided Bird with his most anxious moments. Kim Hughes, Australia's captain, attempted amateur psychology of his own with some mocking gestures in Willis' direction. Willis was goaded into what Bob Taylor, England's wicketkeeper, classified as 'the most blatant no-ball I have ever seen from him' and proceeded to bowl five bouncers in two overs to fuel the umpire's anger.

When Australia passed 100 with six wickets remaining, England's cause looked lost. Willis was exhausted, Botham was not exactly aching to bowl and what little hope there was seemed to rest with the off-spin of John Emburey, who was bowling tightly and intelligently, but who had little history of bowling a side out at Test level.

Brearley, sensing the game was lost, invited Bird to pass an opinion. 'I think you're struggling, Skip,' said Dickie. 'Best thing to do is put the spinners on and that'll get us off early.'

Botham readily agreed. But the next over, Emburey dismissed Border with one that bounced and Brearley was encouraged enough not to take Bird's advice. The plan to call up Peter Willey's off-spin was abandoned and, instead, he asked Botham to summon up one final effort. Botham's belligerent presence seemed to overpower the Australians as the last five wickets fell for seven runs.

* * *

Intimidation was never far below the surface for the great West Indian fast-bowling attacks of the 1970s and '80s, or for Curtly Ambrose, who has extended the line until the present day. Bird has always been very quick to identify fast bowlers' excesses, whether in short-pitched bowling or verbal abuse, and has taken charge of the situation with great determination.

One of his most notable conflicts on the field was with the West Indies' captain, Clive Lloyd, during the Edgbaston Test of 1984. When Bird warned Malcolm Marshall for intimidatory short-pitched bowling, Lloyd flung the ball away and made no secret of the fact that he thought the umpire was wrong. Bird believes that the captain's irritation was largely based upon a misunderstanding.

The West Indians set a unique record that summer. No side, at the time, had won every Test in a series in England, but they achieved their 5–0 'blackwash' in spectacular fashion. A formidable set of fast bowlers – Marshall, Joel Garner and Michael Holding – backed up by the powerful batting of Lloyd,

Gordon Greenidge, Vivian Richards, made up a side of awesome quality and England were incapable of rising to the challenge. Bird, in fact, witnessed England's only consolation of the summer: a three-wicket victory in a Texaco Trophy international at Trent Bridge.

The Edgbaston Test, the first of the series, had begun horrifically when Warwickshire's opening batsman, Andy Lloyd, making his debut on his home ground, took his eye off a wickedly fast, shortish ball from Marshall and was struck on the side of the head. He spent the next 10 days in hospital, suffering from blurred vision. It was a sickening incident and Bird, badly shaken, as such a sensitive man was bound to be, had no wish to witness a repeat.

The West Indies, by scoring 606 at better than a run a minute, had established a first-innings lead of 415 soon after lunch on the third day. England's top order was again overwhelmed, this time by Garner, before Botham's compulsion for the hook shot tempted Marshall into a diet of short-pitched balls, many of which were greeted by cat-calls from an Edgbaston crowd still bitter at Lloyd's injury.

Bird's warning caused Marshall to complain that he would have done nothing if Botham had struck the ball for six. Marshall then kicked the ball towards the boundary, whereupon The World's Most Famous Umpire told him to go and bring it back again! In spite of their row, Marshall's high opinion of Bird did not waver. 'He is a great character and a first-rate umpire,' he wrote later. 'I have no doubt that he has never made a decision when he hasn't had the game's interests at heart.'[27]

Mike Carey, a committed local league umpire himself, praised Bird in *The Daily Telegraph*, for proving that 'whatever may go on elsewhere does not apply in this country'. That view, however, was not shared by *The Times*' cricket correspondent, John Woodcock, who took offence at Bird's intervention:

'It took Bird, the umpire, to put the West Indies out of their stride ... Seeing that Botham seemed to have a death wish which entailed him being caught at long leg, Marshall bowled bouncers at him so that he might accomplish it. Bird interpreted this as "intimidation", although no-one seemed less intimidated than Botham, who was perfectly happy to swish away until he got out. More often than not, I think umpires are dilatory in invoking the law as it applies to fast, short-pitched bowling, often seriously so. Now, for once, they acted prematurely ... Marshall's bowling at Botham was intimidatory, not tactical. From his reaction ... Lloyd thought so too.'

Law 42.8, although quite specific, remains the most contentious two paragraphs in the rules of the game, largely because it relies upon the interpretation of the umpire: 'The bowling of fast, short-pitched balls is unfair if, in the opinion of the umpire at the bowler's end, it constitutes an attempt to intimidate the striker.

'Umpires shall consider intimidation to be the deliberate bowling of fast short-pitched balls which by their length, height and direction are intended or likely to inflict physical injury on the striker. The relative skill of the striker shall also be taken into consideration.'

Bird later clarified his action. His prime intention had been to protect not Botham but the non-striker, Paul Downton. He had intervened when he did because he considered things were getting out of hand: 'At least I was being consistent. I've always been very hot on intimidation and I warned Malcolm because he had gone round the wicket to Paul Downton in his two previous overs and he was obviously trying to soften up Paul. Ian Botham was on strike when I spoke to Malcolm and, although Ian never minds bouncers, it was getting out of hand. The West Indians weren't too happy about it, but I was applying the letter of the law.'[28]

Lloyd has always been implacably opposed to Bird's stance on intimidation. 'Dickie Bird said he thought we were bowling too many bumpers,' he said. 'That's not acceptable. It's ridiculous. The short-pitched ball is the bowler's surprise weapon. If he is restricted to one an over, once he has bowled that ball, the batsman knows that's it ... Bird said something like "space the bouncers out". I don't know what that means. A lot of these things wouldn't be said if batsmen could handle the pace. They bowl bouncers to us. We hook them for four, or our batsmen get out trying the hook shot. We don't complain. They can't handle pace. That's why they complain.'[29]

At the end of his career, Bird's reaction to intimidatory bowling was as strict as ever. The West Indies fast bowler Courtney Walsh, no longer as slick as he had been at his peak, still incurred his displeasure during the 1995 Old Trafford Test. It was a necessary intervention, England's batsmen having to withstand pace-bowling as ferocious and uncompromising as any they had faced since Antigua five years earlier. Graham Thorpe, whose 94 was an innings of great fortitude, said: 'Walsh was just told to space them out, so I got one near the start of the over and one near the end. I didn't get too far past the front crease.'

By now, Bird was operating under an experimental regulation that had been added to the existing Law 42.8. It sought to clarify the umpire's authority, with bowlers being limited to two short-pitched deliveries an over. The umpires, by and large, did not welcome the limitation, preferring to rely on their own judgement, but freedom to act on their own initiative had gradually been eaten away over Bird's career. Wherever possible, umpires now acted along clearly laid-down guidelines – and a simple limit of two short-pitched balls an over left no room for confusion. A feeling for the game was becoming less important than strict adherence to the letter of the law.

One of the most bizarre moments involving the intimidation law was the occasion when Bird had no option but to no-ball England's left-arm spinner Phil Edmonds. It was during the first Test against New Zealand at the Oval in 1983. England, dismissed in their first innings for 209, reduced New Zealand to 41 for five before becoming held up by Richard Hadlee's resistance in the middle order. Hadlee's nonconformist southpaw batting style was not to Edmonds' taste and, as an expression of his disgust, he bowled him a bouncer. However much of a surprise, and however typical of Edmonds' assertiveness, it could hardly be deemed to have put Hadlee's health at risk. The New Zealander's response was to goad Edmonds further by striding towards him and prodding the pitch a good deal nearer to Edmonds' end than his own. That peeved Edmonds still further and he followed up with a second bouncer. It was all frivolous, if entertaining, stuff, but it left umpire Bird in an unfortunate position. The intimidation law had been further propped up in that series with an experimental limitation of one bouncer per over. Bird had no option but to signal no-ball and issue the baffled bowler with an official warning for intimidation.

Bird's unbending attitude against intimidatory bowling was not just reserved for Tests. His consistency extended to county matches, as the former Derbyshire captain Kim Barnett can testify: 'For such a jovial character, he was hot on intimidation. I remember him warning Devon Malcolm in the first over of a match. It was on a bouncy track at Trent Bridge and Devon had let three bumpers go before anyone could catch their breath. We were very nervous about it because it was in Devon's early days, when we just used to encourage him to run in and bowl as fast as he could. Where it pitched was not very predictable. I think we brought his spell to an abrupt end before Dickie could get any more worked up about it.'

Bird was particularly anxious to protect the lower-order batsmen, regularly nagging high-class fast bowlers to dismiss batsmen of few pretensions through skill rather than fear. Barnett again provides an example: 'We were playing Northamptonshire at Chesterfield in 1991, with Ian Bishop rushing in for the kill, when Nick Cook came in to bat. The first ball whistled past his shoulder and the second flew past his ear, at which point Dickie naturally decided to intervene. "Can this man defend himself, captain?" he shouted across to me. "I don't know, Dick," I replied. "I think we're going to find out." "Not with me umpiring, you're not," he yelled. "First warning!" I always reckoned that Dickie – along with Alan Whitehead – was one of the toughest umpires around when it came to intimidation. What mattered was that he was consistent. You always knew what you were going to get. If you couldn't read how Dickie was going to react after all that time, you shouldn't really have been in the game.'

Bird can at least console himself that he never met a player with a bullying nature to match W.G. Grace. It was a rare umpire who had the courage to withstand such an influential figure. One story relates the time that Grace, still grouching at his soft dismissal earlier in the day, struck a batsman on the pads and, while the umpire was vacillating over his decision, boomed out: 'To the pavilion with you, Sir.' The batsman duly went.

*   *   *

Bird was deeply proud of his record of standing in the first three World Cup finals, so it caused him understandable disappointment when he realised that England's qualification for the 1987 final in Calcutta (where they were to lose to Australia) would prevent him from extending his record. The organising committee had assured him that he would be umpiring the final, and so strong were the assumptions that it would be contested by India and Pakistan that Bird's protestations along the lines of 'But what happens if England get there?' were waved aside. Their reaction enabled Bird to cling to the hope that England's presence in the final would not necessarily prohibit him from umpiring. His integrity, after all, was not in question and his career had begun in an era when English umpires were automatically assumed to be the best in the world.

But cricket was changing. If there was no reason why Bird, as an individual, should not umpire in a final involving England, a more worldly view insisted that his Englishness was ample reason to look elsewhere. Neutrality was not just a question of trust, or individual integrity, it was by now also a matter of nationality. A proposal by Australia's captain, Allan Border, that the final should be officiated by umpires representing the two countries concerned – Bird and Tony Crafter – was rejected out of hand.

'I was very disappointed when they told me I couldn't umpire the final,' Bird said, 'especially as it would have been my 100th international match. While I was very disappointed for myself, I was pleased for our lads. I went into the dressing room to tell them, "You've robbed me of a fourth World Cup final – now go out there and win it."'

Sadly, that proved beyond them. R.B. Gupta and Mahboob Shah officiated in a final won by Australia by seven runs, England's powerful chase of 254 for victory subsiding from the point when Mike Gatting played a reverse sweep at Allan Border's first ball and looped up a gentle catch to the wicketkeeper.

Scyld Berry, cricket correspondent of *The Sunday Telegraph*, commented in *Wisden*: 'If the umpiring was not of the very highest standard, its "neutrality" served to minimise grievances. Poor neutral umpiring, however, can never be a substitute for good umpiring, whether by home or neutral officials.'

Almost a decade later, Berry clearly recalled Bird's disappointment at not standing in the final. 'He had umpired Australia's semi-final against Pakistan in Lahore, and travelled to Bombay in time to see England play India the following day. He was pleased for England, but it was a confusing experience for him. He could not hide his genuine disappointment that they had got in the way of his personal ambition.'

*   *   *

If any cricketing crisis confirmed that umpires were no longer 'the sole arbiters of the game' it was when England's captain, Michael Atherton, was accused of ball-tampering during the 1994 Lord's Test against South Africa. Quite who was the sole arbiter was a moot point: perhaps it was Peter Burge, the ICC match referee, or England's Lord High Everything, Raymond Illingworth. It might have been the BBC cameraman who first focused upon Atherton's 'unfamiliar action' upon the ball during Saturday's play, or the journalists who pronounced so loudly upon Atherton's future. It certainly was not the umpires, Steve Randell of Australia and Dickie Bird.

Atherton was spotted by the TV cameras taking his hand out of his pocket and rubbing it across the surface of the ball. He was summoned before Burge to answer suspicions that he had broken Law 42.5 by using an illegal substance on the ball. Atherton assured Burge that he had not, his offer to allow Burge to examine his trousers was turned down, and his protestations of innocence were accepted.

The following day, as England collapsed to a four-day defeat, further TV pictures provided more damning evidence. Soil could be clearly seen falling off the surface of the ball. The implication was that he was encouraging reverse swing by deceitful means. Illingworth was furious and immediately called Atherton to account. Atherton explained to his chairman of selectors that he did have dirt in his pocket, which he had been using to dry his hands, but that he did not inform Burge because he had assumed that dirt was not classified as an illegal substance. He was correct in his belief that there was no stated prohibition against dirt in pockets, but his actions were unusual, clandestine and therefore suspicious.

Illingworth was determined that England should be seen to take firm action, to placate both the ICC and a frenzied media. He unilaterally fined Atherton £1,000 for carrying the dirt, and a further £1,000 for misleading the match referee. He then settled back to congratulate himself upon the prompt action that had spared Atherton's captaincy. In that assumption, he was probably correct.

Atherton explained: 'I wanted to get one side of the ball to remain dry to help the bowlers to gain reverse swing. I have never worked on a ball to change its condition in my life. Cricketers are allowed to dry their hands on dirt on the pitch. My crime was to pick up a quantity of it, put it in my pocket and dry my fingers that way. It was hot and my palms and fingers were sweaty. When you try to achieve reverse swing you have to keep one side of the ball dry.'

But the storm refused to abate. The country's Know-Nothings (a nauseating band of self-publicists whose vociferousness on major issues is in direct proportion to their ignorance) had a field day. Many in the media were also clamouring for action. Some alluded to methods where soil is not a drying agent but is packed into the heavy side of the ball to exaggerate the weight difference central to reverse swing. Jon Agnew, the BBC's cricket correspondent, became the first journalist openly to charge Atherton with ball-tampering. *The Daily Mirror*, which had condemned Pakistan for alleged ball-tampering in England two years earlier, was also forced to adopt a tough line, headlining England's captain as 'The Soiled Skipper'. Atherton retreated to the Lake District to mull over his future, being persuaded that he should brave out the storm after phone discussions with Illingworth and the Lancashire chairman, Bob Bennett.

Amid the clamour, a remark by Richard Hutton, the editor of *The Cricketer*, that judgement was a matter for the umpires and the match referee passed virtually unnoticed. Illingworth expanded on that theme two days after the end of the Test, claiming that the third umpire, Mervyn Kitchen, had spotted the TV pictures on the Saturday and had contacted Bird by walkie-talkie to advise the umpires to keep an eye on the situation. They did so, and had been quite satisfied there was no problem. Therefore the matter should be closed.

'Merv saw the incident and quite rightly spoke to Dickie Bird on their intercom, asking him to look at the ball,' Illingworth said. 'He did and found nothing wrong, and both he and Steve Randell found nothing wrong subsequently even though they inspected the ball several times an over. The players were not aware of this.'

Randell himself recalls a conversation during the tea interval with match referee Burge, who warned them about what the TV pictures purported to show and instructed them to keep a check on the matter. 'We had been oblivious to what might have been going on,' he said. 'It was a case of ignorance is bliss.' By now, the umpires' jurisdiction had long been diminished. The issue had become too large for them alone to handle. This had become a national crisis and their opinions were overshadowed. In the all-consuming TV age, it could be blithely assumed that the umpires were not in possession of the full facts. A bizarre situation had arisen where the umpires had been satisfied about Atherton's innocence, initially at least, but the cameras continued to promote his guilt. Atherton, sensibly, called a second press conference at Old Trafford to expand upon his innocence. He reasserted 'the values of integrity and fair play' and that he had not attempted to alter the condition of the ball. 'At no time in my career have I cheated or attempted to cheat,' he said.

Ball-tampering, in one form or another – whether by the lifting of the seam, by the applications of creams or lip salve to promote swing, or by the roughing up of one side of the ball in the search for reverse swing – had become common practice over the years as umpires accepted that they were virtually powerless to intervene. An occasional brusque warning not to take too many liberties had been the extent of most umpires' admonishments. Umpires, Bird included, were now reaping the consequences of the established tradition of turning a blind eye. The TV eye, however, was never less than piercing.

Ball-tampering had become a contentious issue during the Pakistan tour of 1992 when Wasim Akram and Waqar Younis used reverse swing – a relatively unknown concept in England at the time – to devastating effect and were branded as cheats in the process. The most embittered comments about them sounded disturbingly racist in tone. The rough outfields, dry pitches and concrete perimeters on Asian grounds had provided perfect conditions for reverse swing to be developed. By applying sweat and shine to one side and leaving the other side dry and damaged, bowlers realised that an old ball would begin to swing in reverse – that is, towards the shiny side. At issue throughout 1992 in England, where bowlers were largely ignorant of the practice, was whether this damage to the ball had been achieved by fair means or foul.

Typically, the Test series had been played in an air of mutual mistrust, with Pakistan characterised in much of the English media throughout the summer as little better than a rabble. The presence of Bird and David Shepherd in the fifth Test at the Oval was a relief, although Bird's jokey comments at a lunch engagement about the need for calm became 'I'll Stop The War' (*Daily Mirror*) and 'I Fear Test War' (*Sun*). By the end of the Test, a convincing win for Pakistan, English scepticism about the legality of Pakistan's bowling methods was rife. Bird, though, despite frequent examinations, had had no cause to change the ball.

The storm duly broke during a Texaco Trophy one-day international at Lord's. Crucially, Allan Lamb, the chief prosecutor, had returned to the England side and, while batting, quietly protested to the umpires, Ken Palmer and John Hampshire, about the state of the ball. It was changed at lunchtime, whereafter a carefully-planned leak from the England dressing room scuppered all TCCB attempts at secrecy. From that point on, English officials dealt in innuendo rather than facts and the air of conspiracy grew ever thicker. The third umpire, Don Oslear, increasingly regarded the whole affair as his personal crusade and, upon his retirement, he became one of Pakistan's fiercest critics.

Ian Botham subsequently claimed that, as far back as 1982, Bird had been involved in a ball-tampering incident involving Pakistan. Lamb was hit on the head by Imran and, according to Botham, it was clear that the quarter-seam of the ball had been lifted. Botham went on: 'I took the ball to umpires Dickie Bird and David Constant and asked them to have a look at it, and they were clearly worried by the state it was in. At the end of the over I had a word with Imran about it and he said, rather ambiguously, that the English bowlers might get it to swing a bit more if they "looked after it a bit better". We made a complaint to the TCCB and the ball was taken away, but nothing happened.'[30]

Pakistan's reputation was so sullied in most Western eyes that, in home Tests, their victories were often put down to biased umpiring. In England, entrenched conservative attitudes have done much to delay the introduction of the independent umpire, but the need in Pakistan had become urgent. Imran persuaded the Pakistan Board of Control to employ neutral umpires in the 1986 series against West Indies, and a trouble-free World Cup demonstrated the benefits the following year.

But the obstructive attitude of the English cricket establishment had done much to delay the introduction of the independent umpire, leaving the opportunity for further umpiring disputes when Pakistan toured England in 1987. It was then that their loquacious team manager, Haseeb Ahsan, publicly challenged the appointment of two home umpires, Ken Palmer and David Constant – the latter still not forgiven for a decision he had given at Headingley in 1982.

Reverberations shook the game most powerfully, however, during an acrimonious tour of Pakistan in 1987/8 when England's captain, Mike Gatting, fell into an inexcusable slang-ing match with the Pakistani umpire Shakoor Rana. England's melancholy in Pakistan during the 1996 World Cup, when a jaded side was further assaulted by intense security, a lack of alcohol and entertainment and abuse in the local media (still, they should be used to that) emphasised that the rifts still remain.

*   *   *

Bird's ability to defuse the tensest of situations was illustrated during Pakistan's three-Test tour of the West Indies in 1993, a clash between the two countries widely regarded as the best in the world. Bird was held in similar regard, so much so that both sides had specifically requested that he should stand in the series. He was a safeguard against suspected foul play, an assurance to both sides that the Tests would not only be conducted honestly and fairly, but be seen to be done so.

Pakistan had acquitted themselves well on previous tours of the Caribbean, but this time their performances bordered on

the disastrous. Still seething from the ball-tampering allegations levelled against them in England the previous summer,
they had dropped Salim Malik, Wasim Akram looked stale,
and Javed Miandad and Mushtaq Ahmed were both troubled
by injury. But it was an incident in Grenada, their last port of
call before the first Test, that really undermined Pakistan's
chances. Four players – captain Wasim Akram, Waqar Younis,
Aqib Javed and Mushtaq Ahmed – were arrested on a beach
late at night and charged with 'constructive possession' of
marijuana. The players complained of rough handling and
ridicule from both onlookers and police officers. Pakistan's
manager, Khalid Mahmood, was of a mind to cancel the tour,
claiming that the players lacked both the physical and the
mental reserves to play the series. Wasim was unwilling to
concede, although his anger was undisguised. 'We are accused
of things wherever we go,' he said. 'Last year in England it was
ball-tampering and now this, which was 20 times worse. We
are not bad human beings. We do not make trouble. All we are
is good cricketers. Why are some people jealous of that?'

The first Test in Trinidad was delayed for 24 hours, until 16
April, and as Bird flew in to take charge of the first two Tests,
he must have been wary of the difficulties he might face.
Instead, the Tests passed off without much in the way of flare-
ups between the sides, other than a petulant kick at the West
Indies captain, Richie Richardson, by the greenhorn Pakistani
seam bowler Ata-Ur-Rehman in the opening Test. That incident
was quickly passed on to the match referee, Raman Subba
Row, for deliberation and Richardson received an official
apology from the bowler. The West Indies, by virtue of victories
in the first two Tests, took the series 2–0 and the peaceful
manner in which it was conducted thereafter was further
testimony to Bird's man-management skills.

'It was fortunate that there were two good umpires in the
series,' said Mike Selvey, cricket correspondent of *The
Guardian*. 'Steve Bucknor is unflappable and the presence of
Dickie as a neutral official was also very positive. There is no

question that it helped to persuade the Pakistanis that whatever problems and prejudice they might be experiencing off the field, life was at least going to be fair during the game.'

Bird did, however, have a most startling hand in the establishing of a new world record. Widely assumed to be the Test umpire least likely to give an lbw decision, Bird, together with Steve Bucknor, gave 17 leg-before decisions in the match, beating the previous record, 14, set in Faisalabad 15 months earlier when Pakistan met Sri Lanka.

It had been a hectic winter for Bird, beginning with the breaking of droughts in Zimbabwe, establishing a world record number of lbws, and finishing in mid-February with a minor flap over the manner in which the final Test in Antigua was abandoned. Tony Cozier, the foremost West Indian cricket writer, was clearly unhappy in the following morning's *Independent*: 'Pakistan's Test series against the West Indies came to an unsatisfactory and controversial end [in St John's, Antigua] yesterday when the English umpire Dickie Bird unilaterally abandoned the last day's play without consulting his colleague, Steve Bucknor. Bird, 60, made his decision after heavy overnight and early morning rain had saturated the outfield. But it was taken half an hour before the scheduled start, by which time the ground was bathed in bright sunshine. The decision surprised Bucknor, the Jamaican who stood in last year's World Cup final in Australia.

'According to the ICC match referee, Raman Subba Row, Bucknor could not be located at the time. Subba Row said he and Bird talked to the management of both teams and Ken Isaacs, president of the Antigua Cricket Association, before Bird officially called play off. "Everyone agreed it was a common-sense decision to call it off early rather than go on for the rest of the day and wait for a possible start after tea," he said. Subba Row claimed that they had searched for Bucknor for "about half an hour".

'In fact Bucknor was in the press box, having told journalists he and Bird had agreed to a further inspection of the ground after lunch, when Subba Row appeared to announce the abandonment. Bucknor seemed understandably bemused but said only, "What can I say? The decision has already been made." He did reveal, however, that he would be clarifying his position in a letter to the West Indies Cricket Board of Control. The result of the match, which was heading for a draw, was clearly not affected but the manner of its abandonment embarrassed Bucknor and called into question the role of the match referee in such circumstances.

'According to the laws, the umpires "shall be the sole judges of the fitness of the ground, weather and light for play". But it was obvious that Subba Row had involved himself in the decision, which will, quite apart from anything else, be seen to have been taken by two Englishmen with no knowledge of local conditions and as a snub to the eminent West Indian.'

Bird threw a calmer light on the matter, suggesting that all parties had agreed there should be no play before lunch and, in the event of further rain, it would be called off altogether. After a brief shower, that decision had been taken, and even then only after discussions with both captains and officials of the Antigua Cricket Association. Nobody knew where Bucknor was and there seemed little point in waiting around. Only Bird's high profile, and reputation for being harassed by rain and bad light, gave the story much credence.

*   *   *

The summer of 1977 was dominated by the Kerry Packer affair. It was the biggest revolution in the history of the game as many of the world's best players rebelled against the established order, signing lucrative deals to play in a rival circus surreptitiously arranged by Packer's Channel 9 television network in Australia. The Packer revolution arose from the businessman's anger at failing to win the TV contract to cover Australian Test cricket from the Australian Board of Control. 'Dammit,' said Packer, as his bid was refused. 'I don't know why we don't put on our own Tests.' A formidable project had begun, one which was to split world cricket down the middle. Packer's financial inducements proved highly persuasive in a game where players were disgruntled about their limited rewards. Officialdom might possess a glorious vision of the game's traditions, but the majority of players were more immediately concerned with the inglorious state of their bank accounts.

By the time the story broke in Australia in May 1975, 35 players had already signed contracts in utmost secrecy, including the England captain, Tony Greig, who was masterminding Packer's recruiting operation in Britain. Clandestine meetings between Packer's aides and the world's leading players had become common in hotel rooms, at parties and in secluded corners of cricket grounds. There was outrage throughout England at the defection of so many leading players. However indignantly they professed their loyalty, the likes of Greig, Alan Knott and Derek Underwood had signed up for a rebel tournament set up in direct opposition to traditional Test cricket. The players protested that they were not only securing their own financial future but forcing cricket to provide fairer rewards for future generations. A majority of cricket followers were more concerned with the survival of Test cricket, instantly recognising that the Packer circus could be only a pale imitation of the real thing.

Packer did not only need players, he needed umpires. Bird's marketability made him the chief target, and he was approached on 17 June, the second day of the Jubilee Test between England and Australia at Lord's. He was promised a reported £75,000 and was left to consider the implications. Bird had never been a wealthy man and Packer's payout would have secured his financial future. He never doubted that he would turn the offer down, but he made himself ill fretting about it.

Six days later, Packer stormed out of an ICC meeting at Lord's having failed to reach a compromise with the cricket authorities, chiefly failing to win guarantees that he would be given exclusive TV rights to Australian tests in the future. That smacked too much of blackmail. By now, he had more than 50 players, including an entire West Indies side. 'From now on, it is every man for himself and let the devil take the hindmost,' he raged to the assembled media waiting outside.

A recognition that attitudes were hardening was enough for Bird to refuse Packer's overtures. Every profession of loyalty was highly prized by the TCCB and maximum publicity was achieved by announcing Bird's decision at Lord's during the Benson & Hedges Cup final, in which he was officiating, exactly one month after he was first approached. The statement, drawn up with the assistance of TCCB secretary Donald Carr, read: 'Dickie Bird has informed the Test and County Cricket Board that he has received and turned down an offer to umpire in the proposed series of international matches to be played in Australia this winter. In coming to his decision Mr Bird stressed strongly his loyalty to English cricket, of which he has been a member for years, and he did not wish to take any action which might be prejudicial to his position as a member of the Test and County Cricket Board.'

The TCCB could hardly have announced a potential publicity coup in stuffier fashion.

By the time that Bird shuffled out to cheers at the start of the Trent Bridge Test, on 27 July, he was more convinced than ever that he had made the right decision. The ICC, at their annual meeting the previous day, had voted to ban all Packer players from Test cricket, a decision that was to be successfully challenged in the High Court on the grounds of restraint of trade at a cost to the authorities of around £250,000. When Knott delightedly completed a century to the applause of the Trent Bridge crowd, Bird expressed what both of them were feeling. 'Knotty, lad,' he said, 'you're going to miss all this when you join the Circus.'

In Bird's home county, his decision was welcomed with particular pride. Traditions were more strongly felt in Yorkshire than in most places, and of the five big names who had shunned Packer – Bird, Geoffrey Boycott, Chris Old, Bob Willis and Derek Randall – three were Yorkshiremen. Whatever the trio's personal motives, a staunch, almost religious belief in the traditional form of the game played a part in their decision. That was particularly true in the case of Bird, who could not loiter in Barnsley town centre for more than a couple of seconds without some well-wisher grabbing him by the arm and commending his loyalty, or enter his front door without being buried by an avalanche of complimentary mail. He was an establishment man, a man who naturally tugged his forelock at authority, someone content to let the game's appointed rulers draw up the guidelines for his career and, indeed, for his life.

'He always called everybody Sir,' recalled Jack Bailey, who was secretary of the MCC (and therefore ex-officio secretary of the ICC) at the time of the Packer crisis. 'There were a lot of Sirs about the place from the minute he entered the room. I suppose it was a sign of respect, although after a while it could become a bit overpowering.'

Henry Blofeld, in his exhaustive study of the Packer affair,[31] touched on the petty jealousies and rivalries that were forever present that summer. A month after Bird had made his decision, Blofeld was having dinner with Packer and Greig in the Dragonara Hotel in Leeds: 'Conversation then turned to umpiring, and Greig said he thought David Constant was the best of the English umpires now that he had the confidence to give a few people out. Packer was interested, and remarked that he had always thought that Dickie Bird had been considered to be the best. Greig said again that in his opinion Constant was the best, and Packer seemed surprised. Greig then leant over the table and said quietly to Packer, "Do you want him?"'

Four years later, Bird proved just as resistant to an offer of £35,000 to umpire a series of rebel tours to South Africa. For all his coaching background in that country, he had not returned since the signing of the Gleneagles Agreement, which barred sporting links with South Africa. 'If the authorities are against us going out to South Africa then that is good enough for me,' he said.

* * *

Ian Healy, the Australian wicketkeeper, has had good cause to consider Bird's qualities. In October 1994, Healy's missed stumping off the leg-spin of Shane Warne allowed Pakistan the one-wicket win which maintained their record of never losing a Test in Karachi. It was one of the most excruciating finishes in Test history, and sounded even more so some months later with the emergence of Australian allegations that Pakistan's captain, Salim Malik, had tried unsuccessfully to bribe them to throw the match. For Bird (who, like all but a handful of players, was unaware of such machinations) to maintain order in such trying circumstances was a redoubtable achievement.

Many pundits studied the TV replay of the fateful, final delivery, as Warne's spin deceived both the batsman, Inzamam, and Healy and wondered whether Bird had signalled leg-byes, rather than byes, out of sympathy for the wicketkeeper. On balance, Healy thinks that Bird's integrity would have overridden any compassion he may have felt. 'I was so numbed by it all that I didn't know at the time what he had signalled,' he said. 'He may have been generous to me, but I think he would have wanted to get it right and would have given what he saw as the correct verdict. Dickie was one of my favourite umpires. He always had a word or two – perhaps saying "well kept" or "you're going well" – and I don't think it's a bad thing that an umpire can behave like that. All our players respected him for that reason.'

After 26 seasons, Dickie Bird's brushes with controversy have been far from excessive, a fact that speaks volumes for his umpiring expertise and powers of man-management. Peter Roebuck certainly thinks so:

'Dickie made his reputation as a not-outer who runs the game well. That ability to defuse the situation rather than become confrontational should not be understressed. He didn't run away from controversies, but he dealt with them. If he hasn't had too many controversies in his career, it is a tribute to his skill. Players won't take liberties with him; they know he is a fair man and don't want to argue with him.'

6

Playing the Game

'If tha's going to play like that, tha'd better not come
back again'
– Arthur 'Ticker' Mitchell, Yorkshire coach, on his first
sight of Bird in the county nets

IT is symptomatic of Dickie Bird's entire life that the greatest
batting performance of a modest career should have become
the source of so much frivolity. Only Bird could have made an
unbeaten 181 for Yorkshire and been summarily left out for the
next game. And only Bird could make so many runs and find
that appraisals of his innings lurch from high praise for a
doughty knock on a difficult pitch to light-hearted remarks
about the number of times he was dropped.

Bird played only 14 first-class matches for Yorkshire and the
1959 season, during which he made that innings of a lifetime

127

against Glamorgan at Bradford Park Avenue, proved to be his last for the county. Calculating that his opportunities would be limited, he spent the next four seasons with Leicestershire, but never recovered from the disappointment at not making the grade with the county of his birth. He made only one further century, against the touring South Africans, before retiring from first-class cricket at the age of 29. He invariably played straight, and his technique was regarded as sound, but his batting was rarely as interesting as his umpiring; it was once memorably described as 'like writing about chess by post'.

To make matters worse, Bird belongs to that rare and unfortunate band whose career runs have actually fallen since his retirement. He had grown used to consoling himself with the respectability of his Yorkshire first-class average: 685 runs at 29.78. There was much distressed clucking when the county's insatiable cricket historians readjusted his figures a generation later to 613 runs at 26.65. If he lives past 100, by then he could find himself in the red.

J.M. Kilburn, the erudite cricket correspondent of *The Yorkshire Post*, liked to present a day's championship cricket as a high-class scholarly essay. Not for him the personality-led pieces preferred today. His evaluation of Bird's unbeaten 181 against Glamorgan seems remarkably low-key nearly 40 years on, but this was an era when Yorkshire success was regarded as the norm. Kilburn, who preferred to deal in cool, detached judgements, was not about to overstate the case. Bird himself might have been overcome by his maiden Yorkshire hundred, but Kilburn prided himself that his own critical faculties remained sharp and unemotional. He wrote:

'The second day was long and confirmatory of general expectations in the accumulation of an enormous Yorkshire advantage. It was a day of distinction for H.D. Bird, who carried his Saturday 48 not out to 181, still not out, in nearly seven hours at the crease. Most batsmen of any ability would probably score 181 being allowed to stay for seven hours, and Bird was allowed to stay through some fielding deficiencies, but the endurance itself involves some merit in physical condition and powers of concentration. Bird's innings had some additional merits, not least of them some impressively firm straight driving ... His batsmanship was, of course, inadequate in its ability to reach dominance after so long an acquaintance with the bowling, yet there is clearly the virtue of determination in a cricketing character that conquers restlessness and rejects the urge to rashness under unwelcome restraint ... If he is not pleased with himself, he is inhuman; if he does not become an improved batsman for the experience, it will be a disappointment.'

Don Shepherd, a member of Glamorgan's attack that day, has had cause to relive Bird's innings on countless occasions, the topic invariably being raised whenever Dickie raises a glass of stout in Wales. 'Dickie wasn't a regular and he wasn't at his best,' Shepherd recalled. 'Some batsmen might have jacked it in out of embarrassment, or a feeling that it wasn't their day. But Dickie just soldiered on. He did a bloody good job. He often recounts that innings when he meets up with the Glamorgan lads. By the end of the night, he gets a bit carried away and says he was only dropped twice, and I tell him it was more like half a dozen.

'We had a bad day in the field. It sounds cruel to say it, but Dickie admits to being dropped a few times and it was probably more than that. Accuracy doesn't really matter any more, though, so it's best to err on the side of kindness. There was always something in the pitch at Bradford, but it was a horrible fielding ground. Looking towards the old Park Avenue football ground, it was always pretty grim, especially when things became a bit dark. But the crowd was very close and intense. There was always an atmosphere. It was a great place to play.'

Long afterwards, Bird admitted only one blemish – 'I were missed once on the boundary and the fielder dived full length and then only just got a hand to it. Someone's got this all wrong. It were Wilson who kept getting dropped. Platty [Bob

Platt], the next man in, were up and down those steps like a yo-yo'[32] – but over the years, he has had to make a few concessions to truth. *Wisden* records drops at 53 and 102.

Understandably, the innings remains a source of considerable personal pride. Park Avenue was never a comfortable ground for batsmen. It allowed runs only grudgingly, with the pitches often damp and responsive to seam and the weather typically dull and overcast. Average totals at Bradford, compared to most other county grounds, were low. There have been numerous examples of giveaway centuries at, say, Scarborough – Bird has had to stand and watch quite a few of them during his umpiring career – but Park Avenue refuses to grant its favours lightly. The spectators at one of the North's harshest industrial cities would have glowered at any suggestion of easy pickings. They preferred batsmen to toil for limited rewards.

Glamorgan's attack, as Shepherd readily agrees, was more than respectable. Alan Watkins, in Shepherd's estimation, 'would have been an England regular in this day and age', a medium-fast left-armer who bowled big inswingers. On more responsive pitches, he would often revert to slow left-arm off the same run. He won 15 Test caps, although by 1959 was nearing the end of his career. Jimmy McConnon was a tall off-break bowler who was surprisingly preferred to Jim Laker on England's tour of Australia in 1954/5, even if injury compelled him to return home early. Peter Walker, an all-rounder, and at the time a left-arm medium-paced inswing bowler, was a third England player that day. That is not to overlook Shepherd, by that time in his career bowling off-spin, a redoubtable performer whose 2,174 wickets for Glamorgan, at 20.95 runs apiece, makes him the leading county wicket-taker never to have played a Test. His tallies of both wickets and matches – 647 between 1950 and 1972 – are Glamorgan records.

It is astonishing how the mere mention of Bird tempts his colleagues into wild exaggerations that would be judged rash if describing any other subject. Don Wilson, who thrashed an unbeaten 35 at number 10, recalled that Bird had not even made his 100 when he got to the crease; in truth, he was around 150. He further recalled that after reaching his 100, Bird 'smashed the ball all around Park Avenue'; in truth, he added 12 in the next 50 minutes. Wilson also calculated that he himself was 'dropped eight times', that Bird, who by then was 'playing brilliantly', was 'panic-stricken' that the innings might soon come to a close, and that the number 11, Bob Platt, became so fed up as catches constantly went to ground again that he went outside to watch proceedings from the bottom of the Park Avenue steps; that sounds more authentic, even if it entirely escaped the cricket correspondent of *The Yorkshire Post*.

Wilson's description of Bird's manner will also cause everybody to nod with recognition. 'Birdy kept rushing up to me and telling me to calm down, throwing his arms out and getting very excitable. Everyone was delighted for Birdy when we came off. He was so uptight and serious about the whole thing that I had to take his gloves off for him. He was shaking like a leaf and crying with the emotion of it all. Maybe the innings did him harm. The side was established, and was contesting championships and Dickie was so emotional about his innings that it was hard to pick him after that.'

When Bird returned to the dressing room, beside himself with excitement, the imposing figure of Brian Sellers, disciplinarian and autocrat, and Yorkshire's chairman of selectors, was there to meet him. Sellers prided himself on his bluntness. 'Well played, Dickie lad,' he said. 'But get thee bloody head down, tha's in't second team next week.'

'Thank you, Mr Sellers,' Dickie responded.

His demotion was not as extraordinary as it sounds. Ken Taylor, an England opener, had missed the Glamorgan match and was available again. Yorkshire's colts were used to filling in as needed and then being routinely dropped to continue their education in the 2nd XI. The small matter of an unbeaten 181 did not mask who was the better player; Taylor's return was automatic. Jack Birkenshaw, a young Yorkshire off-spinner who had bowled them to victory with five for 54 in

Glamorgan's second innings, suffered an identical fate as he was dropped for Raymond Illingworth. Bird played six more first-class matches that season before electing to continue his career elsewhere. Birkenshaw was also soon to move on to Leicestershire, although his links with the county were to prove far more extensive than Bird's; after 20 seasons as a player, he later returned to coach them. Both at least had the consolation of being in the Yorkshire party when the county won the championship in dramatic fashion at Hove by scoring 215 runs in only 96 minutes.

Don Wilson remembers with affection Bird's skills in Yorkshire's team of troubadours. During the off-season Wilson and Phil Sharpe would work as dressers for the *Black & White Minstrel Show* and it was not long before the songs were being crooned around the Yorkshire dressing room. Bird, a lover of such shows, was a friend of Tony Mercer, one of the lead singers, who also came from South Yorkshire, and he enthusiastically joined the routines.

'Dickie's favourite was "Abba Dabba",' Wilson said. 'He was brilliant at it. He was never quite word perfect but the actions were terrific. People used to scream with laughter as he did all the lines about the monkey and the chimp. He used to call it "my big baboon act". It became so well known when we were coaching in South Africa that Eddie Barlow still calls him "Abba Dabba". Dickie enjoyed good company. He didn't get drunk, but he used to down lots of cups of tea with enormous amounts of sugar in them. His social life was very much involved with his Mum. The local lasses up my way in Settle used to love him to death, but he never bothered much.'

*   *   *

Leicestershire never worked out for Dickie Bird. Weened on the big crowds at Yorkshire grounds, he described it as 'like batting in a graveyard'. The county was as used to failure as Yorkshire was bred on success. In his first season they won only two matches and, although Bird managed more than 1,000 first-class runs – enough to be awarded his first-team cap – he struggled to come to terms with leaving his native county. In the next three seasons he became even more depressed as injury, including a car crash in August 1962, and poor form prevented him winning a regular place in the side. His most eye-catching moment occurred when he was fielding at Worcester in rubber-soled shoes, slipped on the lush turf as he chased a ball to the boundary and trapped his head between the pickets. The match was held up while a solution was found. 'They had to find a carpenter to get me out,' he hoots.

In total, Bird scored 3,315 first-class runs for Leicestershire at an average of 20.71 and, as Jack Birkenshaw recognised, he never really settled: 'It wasn't always easy to break into a new county. These days, if a new player comes onto the staff, he is encouraged because we all want him to do well and improve the team. It hasn't always been like that in county cricket. There was a bit of resentment among some of the senior professionals whenever a new player arrived. He might be regarded as a bit of a threat to their livelihood. I managed to stick it out but it took me a long time before I felt that I was properly appreciated. Dickie became the butt of the dressing room jokes and he was in a bit of a state because he wasn't scoring runs. He obviously wasn't enjoying it.'

Upon announcing his retirement, Bird took up a coaching post at Plymouth College and became the professional at Paignton Cricket Club. His fondness for the area is still seen in his winter retreats from South Yorkshire to a Torquay hotel. Indeed, he was there when the announcement of his international retirement was made.

'County cricket will be all the worse for the absence of this amiable, schoolboyish, enthusiastic character,' wrote Keith Lodge, in *The Barnsley Chronicle*. 'But it is of the utmost consolation to know that Harold Dennis Bird is not to be lost to cricket altogether. That would indeed be tragic.'

If there was an overriding reason why Bird did not make the grade at county level, it was nerves. John Hampshire, also starting out at Yorkshire about the same time, remembers even having to help him pull his gloves on in benefit matches because he was so agitated. 'I first met him when he played for Barnsley. Rotherham used to have a team called the Rooters – not because of our social habits, but named after a chap called George Root, who was captain of Rotherham Town at the time. Dickie used to play for us. His style was immaculate. He played extremely straight and had a full array of shots. He wasn't particularly powerful but, as an opening batsman in league cricket, he was very difficult to close down.

'One year at the Scarborough Festival, he creamed Frank Tyson through the covers twice off the front foot. The next delivery, he was still going forward when the ball hit him smack between the eyes. That was enough festival cricket! Dickie had great escapades at the festival singalongs with Wilson and Sharpe. He wasn't a singer at all, but he only needed two pints of Guinness and he thought he was Al Jolson. He was always an easy leg-pull. Yorkshire played Ireland in Belfast in 1960 and Dickie had never left England in his life, so they persuaded him to ring up the MCC and ask if they could sort him out a passport.'

Bird concurs with Hampshire's judgement as to why his playing career stalled. 'I'm not being big-headed, but Raymond Illingworth said that no-one played straighter than this bloke with the white jacket on, Dickie Bird,' the umpire once said proudly. 'I thought I had a bit of ability, but I worried too much. It used to affect me as a player.'[33]

*   *   *

Dickie Bird's father never saw him umpire. James Harold Bird worked as a miner at Monk Bretton colliery from the age of 13 and died five years after his retirement of silicosis, a lung disease caused by years of inhaling dust. Crawling through narrow seams to hack out the coal with picks, he would often lose his trousers and work on without them, collecting them at the end of his shift. The mining industry had a proud tradition of supplying Yorkshire cricketers, with more than 20 having links with the industry, including Fred Trueman, Herbert Sutcliffe, Johnny Wardle and Major Booth, who was killed in the First World War. Dickie Bird worked as a fitter at Monk Bretton colliery after leaving school. But he had seen enough; there was no way he was ever going to go down a mine.

James Harold Bird was a decent and moral man and ensured that such attributes were impressed upon his son. It was after attending his father's funeral in June 1970 that Bird called in at Headingley, where Yorkshire were playing Derbyshire, for some much-needed cheer. Doug Padgett, Don Wilson and Barrie Leadbeater were in the Yorkshire side that day. Deeply affected by his father's death, he admitted how much he missed the camaraderie of the county circuit. They asked him if he had ever thought of becoming an umpire. Bird laughed and told them they must be joking. Two months later he wrote to Lord's and before too long received a letter from Donald Carr, secretary of the TCCB, informing him that he had been accepted for the 1970 season.

'At the time, the umpires' list wasn't strong because the money was so poor,' said John Hampshire. 'Dickie was such a nice guy, such an honest guy. His behaviour had always been beyond reproach. He took to it immediately.'

*   *   *

Dickie Bird was born on 19 April 1933. When he was two years old the family moved from their spartan terraced house in Church Lane in the centre of Barnsley, 50 yards from Barnsley Town Hall, to a council house on the New Lodge Estate, which had the luxury of an inside toilet, and he would continue to live there until well into his umpiring career. One of his best friends at school was the great Tommy Taylor, who was to play centre-forward for Manchester United and England. Taylor died in the Manchester United air crash at Munich Airport in 1958. He had been one of the finest headers of a ball of his age, and Bird had seen those skills develop as a youngster, when they would practise late into the evening on a piece of waste ground. Taylor's dad could not afford to buy him a pair of football boots – he used to play in an old pair of plimsolls – so Dickie would cross the ball and 'Tucker' used to head it in.

Bird occasionally teamed up with Taylor in the school football team at Raley Secondary Modern in Barnsley. He was a promising inside-forward, even if he was one of the smallest players in the side. He would often hang around Oakwell, home of Barnsley FC, kicking a tennis ball against the wall while he waited for the players to come out and sign autographs. After leaving school at 15 he signed amateur forms at Oakwell. At that time he had ambitions of becoming a double professional in football and cricket, something which Willie Watson, another Yorkshireman, had achieved with distinction. But, at 17, he suffered a serious knee injury while playing for Barnsley YMCA. He had a cartilage out and had to return to hospital for two further operations. That was the end of Dickie Bird's footballing ambitions.

'He had the physique of a hatpin and the only geriatric stoop I have ever seen on a 15-year-old.' Such is Michael Parkinson's first cricketing memory of Dickie Bird.

Bird had fleeting visions of becoming a fast bowler, but soon settled down to life as an opening batsman. His slight build meant that he lacked power, but he always played straight, got behind the ball and collected his runs by working the ball around. He joined Barnsley CC at Shaw Lane, where Parkinson, a left-hander, occasionally opened the batting with him. By the time Bird had become a professional, at the princely sum of £4 a week, an earnest young man was batting at number six – Geoffrey Boycott.

Barnsley soon obtained a Yorkshire trial for Bird at Headingley, where he came under the demanding gaze of Arthur 'Ticker' Mitchell. According to Bird, he spent 15 minutes batting in a rain-affected net against three England bowlers, Johnny Wardle, Bob Appleyard and Fred Trueman, and failed to hit a single ball. 'If tha's going to play like that, tha'd better not come back again,'[34] growled Mitchell. He did go back again, signed as a professional in 1952 at £12.50 a week and made his first team debut against Derbyshire at Headingley five years later.

* * *

Long-standing members of Paignton Cricket Club have observed Dickie Bird's transformation into a great sporting character with a mixture of delight and incredulity. The Test match umpire confident of his place in the world is a far cry from the solemn figure they recall during his seasons in the south-west. Bird's life was full of uncertainty at the time. His father's hopes of a long and happy retirement after more than 50 years as a miner were blighted by the onset of silicosis; his own county career had ended in unhappy circumstances at Leicestershire. Approaching middle age, he remained a single man unsure of what lay before him.

Ron Fenton, a past chairman and president of Paignton CC, served as captain during Bird's time at the club. League cricket had still not arrived in Devon and, especially in midweek friendlies against touring sides, the teams had to umpire themselves. 'The funny thing was that Dickie would do everything he could in those days to avoid a spot of umpiring,' Fenton recollected. 'He probably thought that, as the professional, if he showed too much enthusiasm for it, he would always be doing it. He was a lot keener about having a net, though. I certainly did my share of bowling to him. It's fantastic to see what he has achieved. We all acknowledge what he has become, but he wasn't the flamboyant character in Paignton that he is now. To be honest, he was a bit dour, not always an easy chap to chat to. He wondered where his life was going. It was of great concern to him. He wasn't really a great socialiser, but he was always good for 50. Everybody used to smile at his broad Yorkshire dialect. We'd love to see him back sometime at another club dinner.'

Benny Hill, a Yorkshire sports journalist for more than half a century, started out at *The Barnsley Chronicle* in 1943 and had graduated to sports editor by the time that Bird broke into the Barnsley side. They regularly grabbed tea together at Redmans, a small coffee bar in the town centre, where they would natter about sport on a couple of high stools over a cup of coffee and egg on toast. According to Hill, Bird has changed little since his teenage years. 'He was never a snappy dresser, he was always a nervous type and he never stopped talking,' he recalled. 'Probably a bit like me, really. He had a typical Barnsley sense of humour. It's different from Sheffield or Rotherham humour, although you foreigners probably wouldn't recognise it. It's a much drier humour all round and Dickie has always possessed it.'

Hill would regularly join the likes of Bird, Boycott, Parkinson and Eddie Leggard (a firm friend of Bird's who went on to keep wicket for Warwickshire) on the Barnsley CC coach travelling to away matches in the Yorkshire League. They were more disciplined times and mention of wild nights out prompted a knowing chuckle.

'None of that group drank much,' Hill said. 'It sounds almost unbelievable now. You know, I was 28 before I had a pint and I entered journalism when I was 16. I've made up for it since, mind. They were a very respectful bunch, too. We once stayed overnight in Scarborough with somebody's auntie, I can't remember whose. There was only one bed and they let me have it because I was older than they were. You wouldn't find that happening now.

'The great thing about Dickie is that he hasn't forgotten Barnsley and he hasn't forgotten the people who helped him when he was younger. There are no airs and graces about him. I was at a sports dinner in Penistone a couple of winters ago when Dickie was speaking. He started off by paying tribute to the work I'd done for sport in the region over the past 50 years. It drew quite a round of applause. I was quite embarrassed by the whole thing.

'He is more astute than people give him credit for and he has looked after himself. Sometimes, even as a journalist, I wonder if he has over-publicised himself a bit, but if he has done so it's not because he's arrogant, it's because he's just so chuffed at what he's been able to achieve. He's as straightforward as they come is Dickie, a real Yorkshireman.'

*   *   *

Dorothy Hyman is one of the finest of the sportsmen and women produced by Dickie's home town of Barnsley. Between 1958 and 1964, as a 100m and 200m runner, she won every medal but one in the Commonwealth Games, European Championships and the Olympics. Only an Olympic Gold escaped her. After 30 years with the National Coal Board, she now works for Barnsley social services, assisting people with learning difficulties.

Over the years, she has regularly attended local sports forums and similar events with Dickie and recognised from the start that he was 'a whittler', a South Yorkshire term for someone who worries. 'I never had to say much,' she said. 'I just used to sit there while he got everybody laughing. He told me that when he played for Yorkshire he couldn't eat for a week because he was so nervous,' she said. 'I'm amazed he has done so well as an umpire. He is so well respected. Mention Dickie's name in Barnsley and people's faces just light up. He has never left the district, just like me, and they probably appreciate him all the more for that.

'He is a Straight John Bull, is Dickie; people feel they can trust him. In sport, more than anything you need to feel that you will get a fair deal. Both our Dads worked at the same colliery and they often exchanged information about us. We have quite a few similarities. Like Dickie, I suppose I might have left the area if I'd ever got married, but I didn't. Some people say we had the odd dance together at Wombwell, but I can't remember that. Occasionally, I still bump into Dickie in the middle of Barnsley. He has such a loud voice that everybody in the town can listen to his side of the conversation. He is very sentimental. He once asked me what I'd done with all my medals. I said that I'd got them all in a frame on the wall. "'Ave yer!" he exclaimed. "Ah've got all mine in t'bank!'"

*   *   *

Wombwell Cricket Lovers' Society, formed in 1951, has gained an unrivalled reputation for the quality of its guest speakers over the years. Nowhere is cricket loved and debated more enthusiastically over the long winter months. By the time Dickie Bird broke into the Yorkshire side, it had become a social institution. Jack Sokell, the society's secretary since its inception, would occasionally invite people such as Bird and Dorothy Hyman to judge beauty contests and to take part in the dances that attracted people from all over the area.

'In his younger days, he enjoyed dances. He was a slim, swarthy figure, even as a teenager, and he was never short of partners,' Sokell said. 'He was always accepted as a genuine lad. He talks about cricket all day, but he has never had a bad word for anyone. They were a bit reluctant to accept Dickie at Shaw Lane. League clubs were quite aloof in those days and Dickie didn't quite fit their image. He turned up for a trial with his kit in a carrier bag and some of them didn't like that. But a fellow called Alf Broadhead recognised his talent and his enthusiasm and looked after him. Dickie came up the hard way and it shows. He will never forget how much Alf helped him. We've all got a lot to thank him for. Dickie has coached several Wombwell lads who have gone on to play county cricket – Martyn Moxon, Tim Boon, Ian Swallow – and he is a good spotter of young players. He still comes to our winter nets today and he is one of our biggest supporters. One of the great strengths that he has as a coach is that he will listen to the lads and consider their problems. He never just lectures them.

'He is a patron of Wombwell now. He has been a member since 1958 and, when he has a chance to return, he always has a good natter and enjoys himself. Our first-ever speaker at

Wombwell was Johnny Wardle, the Yorkshire and England left-arm spinner, and what Dickie learned from him was all about angles of bowling. Wardle made Dickie realise how many balls delivered from wide of the crease would miss the stumps. I think that helped him when it came to giving lbw decisions. He realised that a lot of them couldn't possibly be out.'

And thereby hangs another tale...

7

The Great Not-Outer

'The not-outer is small, wizened, misanthropic, drinks
half-shandies and eats sparingly'
— Michael Stevenson in *The Cricketer*, 1963, on
umpires who don't give 'em out

NORTHAMPTONSHIRE have become accustomed to disappointments in Lord's one-day finals. They have lost five of their last six finals, with only a NatWest Trophy victory in 1992 to ease their pain. But dejection was not their overriding emotion after their NatWest final defeat against Warwickshire in September 1995. There was also considerable bitterness – and it was directed towards Dickie Bird.

Bird's honesty as an umpire is beyond argument, but it is not stretching a point to say that Northants, for a time at least, felt cheated. They seriously considered making an official written protest to the Test and County Cricket Board and, although they eventually shied away from such a drastic move, it would have been surprising if their views had not reached the higher echelons.

Bird's reputation as a great not-outer, specifically when it came to lbw decisions, had remained unchanged for 25 years. It had become part of his trademark and the county circuit had long viewed it phlegmatically. As long as he remained consistent – which he invariably did – there was little point harping on about it. His record and reputation were unparalleled. But Northants' patience snapped as Warwickshire stole a four-wicket victory with only seven balls remaining. Andrew Radd, editor of the county yearbook, received one photograph of the balcony prizegiving, which showed Allan Lamb, Russell Warren, and Alan Fordham glaring at Bird, and instantly thought of captioning it: 'If Looks Could Kill.'

Warwickshire were a daring and inventive one-day side, made so by the resourceful captaincy of Dermot Reeve. They had dominated the domestic game for the past two seasons, but they were losing the match, at 122 for five with 15 overs left, when Reeve came in to bat. Reeve began his innings, according to Nick Stewart in *The Cricketer*, 'as if batting in a fog.' His reputation for driving spin bowlers to distraction temporarily departed as Anil Kumble, the Indian leg-spinner, repeatedly defeated his stroke. One of several lbw decisions looked so plumb, however you looked at it, that even the staunchest defender of umpires suspected that Bird had seriously erred. Even Reeve admitted afterwards: 'I might have been lucky. It was Dickie umpiring, and you struggle to get an lbw decision from him.' There were even allegations that Bird had remarked to Kumble that, if he wanted lbws, he should be bowling at the other end. On occasions when Bird has made such a remark it has been a statement of professional pride, an honest appraisal of his own style. To some Northants players, coloured by the disappointment of defeat, it merely sounded unjust.

Kumble himself, a kindly and discriminating man, is protective towards Bird. 'He might have said something like that, but I thought nothing of it. It's just his way. I certainly saw no reason to become upset about it. I wanted to bowl at Dickie's end because of the Lord's slope, and never thought about switching to try to find a more sympathetic umpire.'

Warwickshire had actually advised their batsmen before the final to use their pads as a second line of defence, more so than is the norm, when facing bowling from the end where Bird was officiating. Dominic Ostler, who was bowled by Kumble's top-spinner, was allegedly criticised for not doing just that.

All umpires are fallible, and are entitled to make mistakes, especially in an age when gamesmanship creates excruciating pressures. But Bird's decision was interpreted by his most trenchant critics in a more critical context, as proof that his reluctance to give lbw decisions had by now become irrational. As the end of the season approached, and he began to prepare for a trip to Australia, where he was to stand in two Tests, opinions began to be voiced that his international retirement was overdue. Australia turned out to be his last overseas tour.

Northants players and officials are apt to dwell upon an earlier incident involving Bird the not-outer. It occurred at Bournemouth in 1988 when Dennis Lillee was refused a shout against Chris Smith in the first over of the innings. Even Lillee, whose respect for Bird knows few bounds, was taken aback not to win the decision. Nick Cook, Northants' left-arm spinner, and a man blessed with a certain eccentricity himself, later responded to the umpteenth lbw refusal by crawling on his hands and knees towards midwicket in feigned desperation. Dickie joined in the joke, although not everybody was laughing.

Umpires are a soft target. One wonders whether Bird will one day attract criticism for some other decisions he has never given. As far as can be ascertained, he has never dismissed anyone 'shambled out', or 'nipt out', or 'hit wicket after remembering what he had forgotten'. He certainly would not dream of following another old-scorebook oddity: 'Given out because the umpire could no longer bear to watch a man in an MCC sweater batting so badly'. Bit of a shame, really.

Jack Simmons, the former Lancashire off-spinner, was invited by Bird to join him coaching in South Africa at the end of the 1971 season. Both were relative newcomers on the county circuit and Simmons, deciding the opportunity was too good to pass up, joined several other county players including Bob Woolmer, now building a fine reputation as South Africa's coach, and Clive Radley, who has since progressed to become head coach at Lord's.

At Heathrow, Simmons broached the painful subject: why had Dickie not given him a single leg-before decision in his first two years on the circuit? Bird informed him that he was bowling too wide of the return crease. 'If a batsman is on the front foot, and it turns, it is probably doing too much and will miss leg stump,' he reasoned. 'Even if it doesn't turn, it will probably still miss leg stump, or else strike the pad outside the line of off-stump so I can't give it out.'

Simmons accepted the argument, and drew an undertaking from Bird that during the winter he would help him get closer to the stumps. They laboured long and hard until Dickie told him that he was in the right position – there was now every chance of the ball striking the pad in line and going on to hit the stumps.

The following season, Bird soon came to umpire at Old Trafford. Simmons, remembering his advice, bowled from close to the stumps, the ball travelled unerringly from wicket to wicket and struck the batsman on the ankle, on the back foot, bang in front. It looked a cert.

'Howzat, Harold Dennis!' Simmons cried with a knowing smile.

'Not out,' said Dickie. 'You got so much in front of the stumps I couldn't see the batsman!' (Simmons checked with several other umpires and found that they confirmed Bird's complaint. He adjusted his style again, and eventually had many more lbw decisions as a result ... including a few from Bird himself.)

There are some to whom Dickie's pride in his lack of lbw decisions could occasionally sound quite bizarre. One former player, who joined the first-class umpires' list in the mid-1980s, was taken aback by a conversation with Bird when they stood together for the first time. 'I walked in around nine o'clock and there was Dickie, already in his kit,' he said. 'He'd probably been there for several hours. I'll never forget his first words to me, they seemed so strange at the time. Most umpires might offer a "Good morning," but Dickie rushed up and said: "Do you know, lad, I never gave you out lbw in the whole of your career." I said something like: "Well, Dick, either you were wrong or the rest of 'em were, because the other 23 buggers did!"'

Bird has not been the only umpire to be resistant to lbw appeals. Alfred Mynn, the 18-stone Kent cricketer, was regarded as the finest all-rounder of his time in the mid-1800s and took up umpiring upon his retirement in 1854. Mynn was so disdainful of leg-before appeals that any bowler summoning up the courage to appeal after striking a batsman on the pads was likely to be met by the abrupt rejoinder: 'None of that. Bowl 'em out.'

Another umpire on the first-class panel considers that Bird's tendency as a not-outer when it comes to lbw decisions has contributed to his efficiency elsewhere. The theory is that by removing much of the need to look for leg-before decisions, by determining that they will be given out only if they are obvious to the naked eye from the back of the pavilion at deep square leg, that allows Bird to commit his full powers of concentration to other areas. To advance this hypothesis openly would invite censure from the TCCB, so it is not surprising that those who agree with it prefer to remain anonymous. But Bird's standing in the game has been so vast that it should come as no surprise that other umpires wish to analyse the reasons for his success. It is not particularly that they wish to carp; it is rather that their urge to achieve the same success, and the same recognition, leads them to wonder whether he has possessed a secret formula.

'Most first-class umpires, if they examined their priorities, are probably looking down the wicket for lbws,' this umpire contends. 'Of course, they are looking for any appeal, as they must, but if they are honest they would probably admit that the lbw decision dominates their thinking. For leg-before decisions, the line of the ball is the key factor. How close is the bowler to the stumps? Where did the ball pitch. Did it swing or deviate off the seam? As far as lbws are concerned, there are an awful lot of factors to take into consideration, all floating around at the back of an umpire's mind. Dickie's mind might have cleared by not looking in particular for leg-before decisions. If you adopt the view that you will disregard every lbw decision unless it smacks you in the face that it is hitting middle stump halfway up, then there is not too much to worry about. It is the one that would have struck the top of leg stump that causes the problems. By disregarding lbws, perhaps Dickie has been able to spot more close-to-the-wicket catches, spotting the faintest edge to the wicketkeeper, or the slightest deflection off the bat to short leg that other umpires might be unsure about. By concentrating upon those sorts of dismissals, he might have been able to pick up more than anybody else.

'Of course, an umpire has to look at the overall picture, that is obvious. But certain priorities do take over. Your knowledge of certain bowlers demands that you are watching out for certain things. If Anil Kumble is bowling, the top-spinner racing into the pads could be along at any moment; for Dominic Cork, you are always expecting an outswinger to take the edge. The way a batsman plays – is he moving too far across his stumps, for instance? – also acts as an early-warning system. It is one hell of an umpire who is capable of giving maximum attention to everything.

'Towards the end, Dickie has been pressurised to give more lbw decisions. It is a changing world and people were beginning to question all his not-outs. Instead of being proof of his immense consistency and fair-mindedness, his decisions began to receive a negative reaction. That caused him to think about adjusting, but he had never umpired like that in more than 20 years, and it was too late to change.'

Bird's consistency cannot be faulted. From the moment his letter arrived from Lord's to tell him he had been appointed to the first-class panel for the 1970 season, he decided he would give a batsman out only if there was not the slightest doubt in his mind. The lbw decision is so riddled with imponderables that to allow only a small proportion could be easily justified. Not for Dickie Samuel Butler's dictum that 'Life is the art of drawing sufficient conclusions from insufficient premises.' He has always claimed that lbw decisions cause him no problem at all – he has only ever given them if the batsman is dead in front of the stumps.

Other decisions have also become more challenging as Bird's career has progressed. Barry Richards once famously remarked that 'The only time an Australian walks is when his car runs out of petrol.' Today, any first-class player who walks (except for the obvious) is regarded as a bit of an oddball. Bob Taylor, the former England wicketkeeper, is one ex-player who regards that as cheating. If cheating predominates, he has argued, it is understandable that umpires are making more mistakes. It is equally understandable if, because of their suspicions, they prefer to err in favour of the batsman.

Twice, at least, on the county circuit Bird has even given a batsman out and then called him back. In 1971, his second season on the list, he initially ruled that the Sussex wicketkeeper, Jim Parks, had been run out by a straight drive deflected onto the stumps by Middlesex's pace bowler John Price, before reconsidering and inviting him to continue his innings. The second occurrence, at Canterbury in 1993, was slightly more controversial. Bird reprieved Kent's batsman Graham Cowdrey after first judging that he had been caught at the wicket fending off a rising delivery from Curtly Ambrose. Cowdrey departed with obvious disgust and was about 15 yards from the boundary by the time Bird changed his mind. Some Northants players were wont to enquire if everyone could have a second go if they complained loudly enough. The most severe criticism came from Charles Randall in *The Daily Telegraph* in a piece that Bird felt so strongly about he threatened legal action. Bird had every right to alter his decision. He must have gone through agonies in the seconds it took Cowdrey to get so close to the boundary edge and it took considerable courage to conclude so late in the day that he had made a mistake and to act to try to right a wrong. He could always console himself with the reflection in Somerset Maugham's *Of Human Bondage* that it is only weak men who take such pride in never changing their mind.

Mike Selvey, *The Guardian* cricket correspondent, likes to relate the story of how he helped to 'transform' Bird's approach. As a medium-fast swing bowler for Middlesex and England, he endured more than his fair share of Dickie's rebuffs when he appealed for lbw. 'There were many times when I felt that certain other umpires would have given a batsman out, but Dickie stood there shaking his head until it was about to fall off. Some of them fizzed a batsman out when he wasn't out, and who is to say which one of them was the most wrong. But Dickie wouldn't put himself on the line. He had a policy of not giving much and he stuck to it. By doing so, he avoided controversy and was marked pretty consistently on the county circuit as a result. There might have been a few red-faced bowlers about, but most county captains are batsmen anyway. Dickie was reckoned to be all right.'

When Selvey bumped into the umpire in the Hilton Hotel in Trinidad, on the eve of the West Indies' three-Test series against Pakistan in April 1993, the old bowler in him decided it was time for a gentle wind-up. He continues the story as follows:

'I think we met outside the lift. I told him that he must be the most frustrating umpire of all time because he hardly ever gave anyone out. I suggested that he must even frustrate himself, turning down appeals until bowlers despaired. "Go on,

Dickie," I said, "just for once have some fun, give 'em all out, you'll never know what you've missed until you've done it." He wasn't quite sure what to make of it, but we parted company happily enough and I never thought anything else about it.'

Perhaps it was Selvey, and not his former Middlesex colleague Mike Brearley, who should have moved into psychology. His jokey entreaty was followed by remarkable scenes, as Bird and the West Indian Steve Bucknor set a new world record of 17 leg-before decisions in the first Test.

Selvey continues: 'The Trinidad pitch was made for lbws. It was pacey and well-grassed and possessed no bounce at all. The quality of fast bowlers in the game – Ambrose, Bishop, Walsh, Wasim and Waqar – forced batsmen onto the back foot and as soon as the ball did not get up, often from short of a length, a batsman was bound to be in trouble. Every one of the 17 looked out. It was remarkable. Dickie had never known a time like it. There was a period of less than two hours – the end of the West Indies' first innings and the beginning of Pakistan's reply – when six lbws were given in quick succession. Dickie's and Steve Bucknor's fingers were shooting up: bang, bang, bang. You had to wonder if Dickie's nerves could possibly stand it. When Dickie was told that there had been 17 lbws in the match, he replied, "Ah, yes, but I only gave seven."'

Selvey was intrigued to discover what sort of mental state Bird was in after such an aberration, and it was not long before the umpire came into view. Bird, by now, was relishing the joke:

'He came rushing up and said, "I thought about what you were saying, you know. I saw the first one hit the pad and I thought, that's out; that's out, that is. I put my finger up and just gave it out. Nobody complained. Nobody said a word. It were wonderful. Every time I saw it hit the pad, I just thought, that's out."

'But that was not all. "I've also been thinking about what you said about not giving you any lbws," said Bird. "I lay in bed last night and had a count-up. I could remember 27.'"

Selvey was rendered speechless – as he was a few nights later at a restaurant in Trinidad where a group got together to celebrate Bird's 60th birthday.

'We were all happy to be there,' Selvey said. 'He's put his heart and soul into the game. He has lived it as much as anyone I can remember. At one point he leant over to me, confidentially, and told me that he had had a recount. He hadn't given me 27 lbws, he'd given me 28.'

Graham Gooch once said of his former Essex and England team-mate Derek Pringle that he loved nothing better than to argue the alternative view. It is no surprise, therefore, that Pringle can present for your delectation an lbw decision that Bird gave him when he, the bowler, did not think it was out.

'He gave Merv Hughes out leg-before to me at the Oval in the final Test in 1989, when I was convinced it was nipping down the legside,' Pringle said. 'After putting his finger up, he swung round to me and said, "You see, Derek, I do give some. Tell 'em, Derek, I do give some, you know." We drew that Test as well, with what amounted to an eighth-choice attack, but we still took a hammering in the series.'

Umpires just can't win. That was the series when John Thicknesse, cricket correspondent of *The Evening Standard*, suggested in *Wisden* that in recent home series 'to consolidate their reputation for impartiality, English umpires have tended to favour the opposition, whether subconsciously or otherwise'. If only Bird had been given the chance to offer a suitably brusque Yorkshire reply. 'No, lad, tha's got t'be off tha 'ead. It weren't that at all. It were that Alderman bloke, he were allus bashing 'em on't pads.'

8

Umpire Superstar

'He was the first umpire to combine the distinct roles of top-flight umpire and music-hall comedian. He was the first Umpire Superstar'

– Matthew Engel, editor,
Wisden Cricketers' Almanack, 1996

DICKIE Bird did not stand in the 1996 World Cup but his status as the world's most recognisable umpire remained unaffected. His announcement of his international retirement early in the year brought an avalanche of expansive newspaper features, BBC Radio invited him to choose his *Desert Island Discs*, and he appeared regularly on light entertainment shows to satisfy television's boundless craving for celebrities.

On the Indian subcontinent, he remained equally fashionable. It was impossible to watch television coverage of the World Cup for long without his face popping up in suitably comical fashion.

After Coca-Cola won sponsorship as the official drink of the World Cup, with drinks intervals marked by a succession of ever-more ridiculous vehicles, Pepsi-Cola responded with an advertising campaign of their own. Under the slogan: 'Pepsi: Nothing Official About It,' it hoped to play on young people's appetite for nonconformity and enlisted many of cricket's biggest personalities, including Sachin Tendulkar, Shane Warne and Dominic Cork, in support.

For an umpire to play a part in such an advertising campaign was highly improbable – as a matter of course, they are representatives of authority. But Bird's appetite for the unconventional was still regarded as attractive to a younger audience and he, too, was invited to travel to India for the advertising campaign. One advert threw together film of a few haphazard antics from the world's top players before switching to a close-up of umpire Bird waving his hands and grinning crazily from behind a set of stumps like a character in *Mad* magazine. Nothing too demanding there. A second advert was rather more surreal: Bird sat behind the stumps at a judge's desk while Sachin Tendulkar playfully placed a wig on his head. When Tendulkar displayed dissent at a refused appeal (Bird's reputation as a not-outer being part of the game's folklore), Judge Bird angrily hammered his gavel into a large block of ice which broke into pieces to reveal a glass of Pepsi. The world's most famous umpire then completed the diversion by raising a glass to his fans and parroting the advertising slogan.

Whether Bird would have chosen to appear in the advert had he been a member of the World Cup panel must be doubted. It was a spot of harmless fun, although those in authority might have viewed it slightly differently, believing that it demeaned his authority. But that is incidental. The point is that Bird, less than two years from retirement age and after more than 25 years of laying down the law, still possessed an exuberance and individuality to appeal to a young audience. No industry is more obsessed with youth than advertising, but Bird was still credited with the ability to sell Pepsi to the world. Clearly, here was more than just a Test umpire. Bird was established, as he had been for nigh on 20 years, as an entertainer.

It has been this ability to act the fool, while retaining the respect of his fellow professionals, that, in the opinion of Matthew Engel, editor of *Wisden Cricketers' Almanack*, makes Bird unique: 'Before Dickie, cricket had supported two distinct traditions,' Engel explained. 'There were umpires of character such as Alex Skelding, Cec Pepper and Arthur Jepson, and there were the top-flight umpires who remained a little bit aloof from such a world – the likes of Syd Buller, Frank Chester and Charlie Elliott. What Dickie did was to bring the two worlds together. He was the first umpire to combine the distinct roles of top-flight umpire and music-hall comedian. He was the first Umpire Superstar.'

Bird's popularity has often revealed itself in strange ways. As far back as 1977 he was voted Yorkshire Personality of the Year, squeezing Grimsby's Labour MP, Austin Mitchell, a former Yorkshire TV news presenter, into second place. Twelve years on his fame was established worldwide, and he was invited, presumably on the strength of his surname, to judge Britain's annual talking-bird contest at the NEC in Birmingham. Sure enough, Dickie ensured that the event attracted unlikely publicity by complaining that Billy, an Amazon parrot from Aylesbury, had tried to bite him. 'He'd better not bite that finger – that's the one I give 'em out with,' he splurted. Maybe you do, a few bowlers might have retorted, but not often enough.

Bird reappeared at the NEC in 1993 and, sure enough, another calamity occurred. This time his assailant was an Australian cockatoo called Doodle which bit him on the nose and then, to add insult to injury, swore at him. Bird needed a tetanus injection and sported a natty line in nasal plasters for the photographers. 'His attack on me was quicker than a West

Indian fast bowler,' he said. 'There was blood all over the place.'

One tabloid newspaper imagined it would be a good idea to invite Bird to turn fashion expert and pass judgement on a wide range of Panama hats supposedly sweeping the nation, a craze that no-one else seemed to have noticed. Never mind that Bird had never worn a Panama in his life. The world duly learned that the straw in a hat on sale at Simpson's in Piccadilly was 'a bit tough', and that another on sale at James Lock in St James's Street, in London, was 'very classy' but, as the brim turned up a bit at the back, it might expose its wearer to sunstroke in hot climates. Unfortunately, a follow-up feature comparing flat caps at various outlets in South Yorkshire was never commissioned.

Bird travelled the world, willingly agreeing to stage-manage another ludicrous picture. For his first visit to Sharjah in April 1984, for the Asia Cup, he replaced his white cap with a turban and affected to have a lesson in Hindi. When he returned from a coaching assignment in Nigeria, he happily posed for photographs in bright yellow native dress complete with ebony walking stick. He was a natural performer. One man who had recognised this years earlier was Albert Modley, one of Barnsley's greatest music-hall comedians, who was treasured above all for his tramcar sketch. Modley had the same rich, booming voice and also favoured a cloth cap, and when he met Bird he seemed to sense a budding rival. 'Ee, lad, tha's a bit of a character,' he said. 'Tha could 'ave been a great comedian thissen.'

Bird has developed a successful after-dinner routine, in which his staple stories are given the usual overwrought treatment. If England ever tires of hearing them, his Australian counterpart, Steve Randell, reckons that he has a ready market in Australia. 'I was invited with Dickie to a big cricket dinner in Sydney last year,' he said. 'Dickie wasn't on the official speakers' list, but he was persuaded to do a few minutes. It was all new stuff to us. The place just fell apart. He'd kill 'em if he did a nationwide tour over here.'

For such a vulnerable figure Bird has rarely fallen foul of the media, even if suggestions in later years that he was on the decline hurt him enough to bring several threats of legal action. For the most part there has been a reluctance even among journalism's most cunning minds to take too much advantage of such a straightforward and harmless character. *The Guardian*'s Mike Selvey does remember one occasion – a lunch thrown by the England sponsors, Whittingdale – when his gullibility did get the better of him.

'It was the year of the Pakistani ball-tampering accusations, and Dickie, as chief guest, was due to give a question-and-answer session after the lunch, everything to be on the record. A few people took him on one side and warned him to be careful, not to say anything daft. At that time, the whole ball-tampering business had run totally out of control. Well, it wasn't too long before Dickie was ploughing ahead, talking about how he was entering a battle zone and how he'd better not forget his tin helmet. He was giving a comic song-and-dance routine to a bunch of cricket journalists. Afterwards, he just said that he thought he was among friends. In many ways he was, but it was a pretty innocent view to take.'

Bill Alley brought considerable entertainment in England for 25 years, firstly as a bold left-handed batsman for Somerset (he played from the ages of 38 to 49) and then as a first-class umpire who stood in 10 Tests until his retirement in 1984. The last regular Test umpire before Bird to retire from the fray, his opinions have remained as bluff as ever in spite of the passage of time. He believes that Bird's like will not be seen again.

'I think that Dickie is the final personality umpire,' he said. 'Dickie adopted the personality thing and took it up in a big way. Whoever follows him will not be able to be so extreme. The game has become far too serious for that. Every time I've seen Dickie on the TV, he seems to be crying. When he got his medal from the Queen, he nearly had a heart attack he was so happy. He's a funny old fellow. When he finished umpiring for the day, it wasn't often you could persuade him to come with you for a drink. He's never been much of a drinker. If we walked into a guest room after a day's play, and I had a large gin and tonic while Dickie had an orange juice, I used to wonder how many people reckoned I wasn't taking the job seriously. Dickie was a character, but he always gave the impression that he was taking the job seriously. I was taking it just as seriously as he was, but it didn't mean I couldn't have a drink.'

Alley was part of a boisterous group of personality umpires who dominated the county circuit when Bird's career began. All of them – Alley, Arthur Jepson and, in particular, Cec Pepper – differed from him in that they were primarily anti-establishment men. Alley's umpiring style was the antithesis of Bird's. He once told Billy Griffith, a former secretary of the MCC, that he had had two ambitions in his life: firstly, to play for Australia; secondly, to become the first umpire to give out all 10 batsmen lbw in a single innings. 'I told him that I'd missed out on the first, but I damn well wasn't going to miss out on the second. He laughed, so I asked him why he was laughing.' On another occasion, he announced that he still harboured aspirations of umpiring an England v Australia Test at Lord's alongside Pepper, a fellow Australian and brash mate. 'Oh, no!' exclaimed Griffith, 'we could never have that.'

Alley failed in all these aims, although he did once give three Leicestershire players out lbw in a Lord's final, which predictably did not endear him to the authorities and which led Raymond Illingworth, then the Leicestershire captain, to suggest that he would never get another Lord's final. Illingworth's prediction was to prove absolutely right.

According to Alley, Bird's meteoric rise to the top of his profession did not find favour with Pepper, who bore too much ill-will over his own unfulfilled career because of his outspokenness and enthusiasm for giving people out. 'Cec Pepper left umpiring at the end of the 1970s because he couldn't understand how Dickie Bird had become the number one umpire in England,' Alley claimed. 'He said that openly, time and time again. He reckoned anybody could stand there and give a player "not out".'

There have been few more forthright characters in cricket than Pepper, either as a leg-break bowler for New South Wales, as a prolific performer in the Lancashire leagues or as a first-class umpire. As Christopher Martin-Jenkins succinctly put it, he was 'a victim of his own impetuosity in an era when a loud mouth was not tolerated'.[35] Pepper's crime was an uncouth comment to umpire Jack Scott after he had been refused an lbw appeal against Don Bradman in Adelaide in 1946. An apology which he arranged to be sent to the Australian Cricket Board never arrived. An exhaustive biography of Pepper by Stephen Thorpe (sadly as yet unpublished) makes light of his supposed resentment at Bird's progress, merely recording that the Australian would occasionally chide Bird for his establishment leanings. His retirement owed as much to his feeling that the fun was going out of the game. There was, though, no disguising the general chip on his shoulder. 'To be a good umpire, you have to be a good not-outer,' he said indignantly. 'Umpiring at the top now is full of comedians and gimmicks. In the old days there used to be men you could respect.'

Pepper claimed that the first advice he had received from Charlie Elliott was that if he wanted to advance his career he should 'look after' the captains; they were the men, after all, who marked the umpires. 'I never condoned that,' Pepper said. 'I used to shoot them out whoever they were.' Batsmen indulging in excessive pad play (before the law was changed, padding up was rife in the late 1960s) were a particular irritant. 'Three kicks and you're out,' he would tell them brusquely. It was no idle threat.

Unlike Bird, who rarely drinks more than a glass or two of Guinness – or these days an occasional red wine on a Sunday to help his circulation – Pepper's idea of fraternisation with the players extended into many lengthy sessions in the bar. Such a hale and hearty approach, according to Thorpe, was instrumental in the Australian never graduating to the Test circuit. One Lord's administrator, Donald Carr, told him as much, leaving Pepper to scowl regularly thereafter: 'I never could be a "yes man" for Carr.'

Pepper did leave a great fund of stories, such as the time at Worcester, during the petrol crisis, when a university batsman thick-edged John Inchmore to third man and Younis Ahmed allowed the batsmen to run three. Inchmore was livid, until Pepper witheringly remarked that Younis probably did not know the speed restrictions had been lifted. Neither did he have much time for helmets. Another story unearthed by Thorpe concerned Dennis Amiss' appearance at the wicket in a Warwickshire v Kent game with a helmet. Pepper enquired where he had parked his moped, whereupon Amiss requested that the umpire hold the helmet when he, Amiss, was at the non-striker's end. 'You hold it, mate, and use it as a pisspot,' Pepper is credited with replying.

Pepper must have been a terrifying partner for Bird's first-class umpiring debut, Surrey's match against Yorkshire at the Oval in April 1970. Bird, as we have seen, had tried to gain admittance in the early hours by scaling the perimeter wall, and must have wondered if he had alighted in a penitentiary by mistake. The weather was discouraging for much of the match but, at one stage, Bird summoned all his courage and ventured to Pepper that a resumption might be in order: 'You suggest nothing, you sit there,' came the reply.

It is inconceivable that such a principled, yet vulnerable, figure as Dickie Bird could have succeeded as an umpire in cricket's earliest days. Outbreaks of violence between rival teams, or their drunken supporters, were not uncommon as large bets were laid on the outcome of matches. Even some umpires were not averse to a bet themselves, especially as they were handily placed to assist in its successful outcome.

One of the earliest flare-ups took place in a match between Kent and Surrey in 1762. One hundred guineas rested on the result, plus a far greater sum in other private bets. But the match remained undecided when an umpire's ruling that a batsman had been caught out caused a storm of protest and involved him in a brawl. And they talk about deteriorating behaviour of modern professionals!

The word 'umpire' comes from the Old French *nomper*, meaning a third person called to decide between two others. That is enough to strengthen some people's conviction that talk of 'neutral umpires' is tautological – all umpires, by their very nature, are neutral. But there was little doubt that when neutral umpires were first introduced in English county matches in 1863 – fees amounting to £5 a match – the standing and dignity of umpires were improved. The same was true when the system of independent umpires was introduced into Test cricket more than a century later, even if some traditionalists felt that the umpires' independence, which should have been taken for granted, had been undermined.

Ever since the throwing controversy in the middle of the 19th century, umpires have been charged with arbitrating upon the game's stormiest issues. Cricket's natural conservatism ensures that change comes slowly and that, by the time governing bodies get around to implementing new laws or regulations, umpires have been placed in demanding situations. One of the first umpires to thrive upon controversy was 'Honest Will' Caldecourt, born in 1802, a former ground boy at Lord's, who waged a one-man resistance against overarm bowling. Perhaps two-man resistance would be more accurate, because with a nickname like that, he clearly had a good PR officer at his side – William Denison, arguably the first cricket journalist of repute. Even at the height of his popularity, no-one ever referred to Honest Dickie, Defender of the Faith.

Caldecourt preferred the Napoleonic pose – one which, if attempted by Bird, might give the impression that he was auditioning for a role in a new *Carry On* movie. A tricorn hat and a hand tucked into a great-coat completed the image. It was 1859 by the time MCC ruled that bowlers should be allowed to raise their arms as high as the shoulder, a decision which helped to persuade Caldecourt to give more time to his bat factory in north London.

Alex Skelding ensured a continuation of the Caldecourt line. Skelding's fast-bowling career at Leicestershire had innumerable false starts, in part because he needed spectacles, a rare sight among players at the time. He stood as a first-class umpire between 1931 and 1958 – a period of office exceeded only by the great Frank Chester – and was the ripe age of 72 when he finally retired. Skelding's wisecracks earned him the nickname of the Prince of Kidders and some county captains believe that he was kept on the list for several seasons after his judgement was waning because of the entertainment he provided. (Bird, by heeding advice that it was the appropriate time for him to retire from international cricket, saved himself from a similar clowning finale.) Predictably, aggrieved batsmen were occasionally moved to question Skelding's eyesight. One of the most famous exchanges concerns the offended batsman who enquired: 'Where's your guide dog?'

'I got rid of him for yapping,' said Skelding, 'just like I'm getting rid or you.'

Skelding was instantly recognisable, with his bulbous nose and white hair, and his preference for bellowing his ruling upon appeals so loudly that they could be heard from the boundary edge. The age of radio was taking hold and Skelding's theatrical ways soon captured the attention. His habit of signalling to the scorers with tic-tac signals (he liked a bet on the horses) and warming himself in the early season with comforting swigs from a hip flask also added to his public appeal. But Lord's, while happy for his extravagances to run unchecked on the county circuit, understandably thought it wise never to offer him a Test match. It is doubtful whether he would have found video replays for close run-out decisions to his taste. Instead, he would stand erect and pronounce: 'Gentlemen, it is a photo finish, but as I have neither the time nor the equipment, it is not out.'

Skelding also dabbled as Leicestershire's scorer for a season, although he was not cut out for such a meticulous task and cared not whether his occasional confusion became public. On one occasion he stuck his head out of the scorebox and beckoned to a small boy in the crowd. 'Go and buy an evening paper,' he instructed, pressing a coin into his hand. 'We'll get the score from that.' At least, that is how the story goes. As with Bird, stories about Skelding habitually weave fact and fiction.

When Skelding gave the Australian Syd Barnes out in 1948, Barnes was incensed enough to make the usual gibes about spectacles and guide dogs. Skelding responded by writing a note to Barnes, explaining that he had three pairs of glasses (one for sixes, one for leg-byes and one for leg-before decisions), but that his guide dog was barred from cricket grounds. Sure enough, fate intervened, as it assuredly would have with Bird, as during the Oval Test a dog raced across the outfield and was apprehended by Barnes. 'Thought your dog never came to the cricket,' Barnes shouted. As well as being an eccentric, Skelding had a keen knowledge of Leicestershire's underworld. On one visit to Grace Road, Sir William Worsley, father of the Duchess of Kent, who served during his lifetime as both captain and president of Yorkshire, had a gold watch stolen. With the help of Skelding's local contacts, the watch was returned the following morning. Skelding's popularity earned him a benefit match, not that he became rich from it. As he later wrote scathingly: 'Play began in a biting wind before a sparse crowd.'

Frank Chester was a representative of the less obtrusive, more considerate breed, and is widely credited with taking umpiring to new heights. In his heyday, he stood in all five Tests in a series, with the rest standing alongside him in rotation.

He was still a teenager when he lost his right hand in the First World War, so ending his chances of forging a successful playing career with Worcestershire. In 1922, still only 26 years old, he took up umpiring and his relative youth, plus his immense sense of loss, ensured that he gave the job meticulous attention.

Chester remained a first-class umpire for 33 years, and his record of officiating in 48 Tests survived until 1992, when it was beaten by Bird in Bulawayo (Zimbabwe). Chester preferred a stooping stance, believing that by lowering his head over the top of the stumps he was better placed to judge lbws. He tended to ponder over his decisions, and was widely respected, even if his reputation as a bit of a stickler occasionally inspired accusations of pedantry. Bill Bowes, the England bowler who formed part of the 1932/3 bodyline attack against Australia, recalled: 'With Frank as umpire, number 11 can be sure he will get the same impartial treatment as the greatest opening batsman. He has earned and deserved the title of "the man who never made a mistake".'[36] How Bird must sometimes wish he had officiated in such gentler days. In such a context, Chester's famous pronouncement: 'Doubt? With me there isn't any doubt,' does not seem quite so indefensible.

While Chester admired cricket's traditions, he could not always be certain of support from those empowered to run the game. At least two major England cricketers, Jim Laker and Sir Leonard Hutton, remembered that during the 1951 Trent Bridge Test between England and South Africa, Chester informed Sir Pelham Warner, one of the most influential figures in MCC history, that in his opinion the South African fast bowler Cuan McCarthy was throwing. He sought assurances that if he did no-ball McCarthy he would be supported by the MCC. Chester, according to Hutton, was told that if he called McCarthy he would probably lose his place on the Test panel. Laker recalls that Warner was troubled by the possibility of 'offending friends' – a disgraceful attitude, if true. After lunch Chester abdicated responsibility at square leg and would not even watch McCarthy bowl. He had chosen career above conviction.

In his later years, Chester's popularity waned a little, in particular among the Australians, who suspected he had become star-struck. That accusation may have been encouraged by Chester's oft-stated belief that England's bodyline tactics – the short-pitched fast-bowling aimed at a batsman's body, employed by Douglas Jardine's side in Australia in 1932/3 – were perfectly acceptable. But Chester also expected decorum on the field, and when Australia toured England in 1948, winning four of the five Tests, he had publicly rebuked them for their belligerence.

As televised cricket became increasingly common, Frank Lee retained Chester's approach and ensured that umpires gained a reputation, on the field at least, for absolute sobriety. But Chester himself was becoming increasingly unreliable. The 1953 Australians complained bitterly of bias, relating that Chester treated them to silence while standing at square leg, although chatting happily to England players when they were in the field, and that he also developed the habit of refusing appeals in an Australian accent. After a below-par Test at Headingley, when Reg Simpson and Denis Compton were both assisted by debatable decisions, Chester was stood down by Lord's on the grounds of ill-health.

Perhaps the most esteemed of umpires directly before Bird arrived on the scene was Syd Buller, who fits into the more serious-minded school of officials. Barry Dudleston, who graduated to umpiring after a successful playing career with Leicestershire, Gloucestershire and what was then Rhodesia, and whose links with southern Africa are still seen in a flourishing sports-tour business in the region, summed up: 'Syd Buller's mystique was that he would never talk to anybody. He preferred long silences, and he was so revered that nobody would ever think of talking to him. If he gave me out caught, I would think that I must be out, even if I hadn't felt anything. He never became a human being, nor felt that he had to be. He was Syd Buller the Great Umpire. Nobody questioned his authority. It's different now – some of them like you and some of them don't.'

Bird's retirement will remove a good deal of character from the umpiring ranks and he may well prove irreplaceable. Umpires are becoming more uniform with every passing year as the search intensifies not just for individual consistency but for collective consistency. When technology is the final arbiter, there is little room for originality. Distinctiveness is more likely to be suspected as a potential threat to an umpire's quality and efficiency. Bird's unconventional behaviour has become deeply loved in the game, but he developed his style when cricket was desperate to promote and enrich itself. Now, more financially secure, it may be less willing to take the risk.

Peter Roebuck reflects: 'Umpires are younger and better trained these days. It is a profession now, not a craft, and inevitably it has become increasingly middle-class. Much of the variety has disappeared. Everyone used to know that it was inadvisable to sweep if Langridge or Budd was umpiring, that Alley could give anyone out at any time, or that Pepper would curse and burp his way through the day. Now people are more cautious in their approach and so their behaviour is more restrained. There are careers at stake.'

Barrie Leadbeater, as a fellow Yorkshireman, has periodically had cause to rally Bird's spirits in his more depressed moments. Leadbeater confidently judges that 'He has been an excellent umpire, respected throughout the world, deserving tremendous admiration and respect.' He recognises, too, that with Bird's retirement the mould may be broken: 'I doubt whether the modern game could accommodate another character like Dickie quite so willingly. These days, an umpire starting out on his career and behaving like Dickie would struggle to make it, in gaining both the acceptance of Lord's and the respect of the players. The game was played more honestly in the 1970s than it is now. There was a lot more fun and a lot more leeway. That was the joy of a professional career. Everybody competed hard on the field, but there was no hint of gamesmanship. There might be the odd word between players, but it was confined to that. Today, people are looking to cheat half the time. It's still not a Them and Us situation, and hopefully it will never come to that; you can still have a laugh and a giggle. But the difference is that players these days – brought up with video replays – are looking for perfection from the umpires. The joking soon stops if they think they've got a bad decision. That an umpire got one wrong occasionally used to be an accepted part of the game. Not any more.

'After a day's play both sides would have a drink and chat together. You don't see that as much now, although there are a few counties that are still making an effort to keep the social side going, and good luck to them.'

If Bird is to be replaced in English affections it will be by David Shepherd, ex-Gloucestershire batsman, who is now widely recognised as the leading umpire in the world. Shepherd's easy affability and portly frame are enough to confirm that he is of a far calmer disposition than his restless predecessor. In place of Bird's maddening collections of tics, Shepherd offers only the curious insistence upon standing on one leg whenever the score reaches 111, the English version of cricket's unlucky number.

The TV cameras, in their insatiable search for colour and character, routinely zoom in while some poor commentator provides an appropriate 'ho-ho, look at David Shepherd' observation. But Shepherd is a less expansive on-the-field character than Bird and, with every passing year, he looks more and more uneasy, as if he privately wishes he had not started the damn business as a player all those years ago. Sometimes, his foot leaves the floor so inconspicuously that there would barely be opportunity to slip a cigarette paper underneath. Imagine if Dickie had developed such an affectation – each leg would be raised to the heavens in turn like a Tiller Girl.

9

The Evil Eye

'The media have set him up as a hero and then kicked him in the arse'

— Bill Alley, former Test umpire

BILL Alley was having none of it: 'Nar, I'm saying nothing about Dickie Bird. Not a single word as long as I live. Everybody wants to know my opinions and I'm telling no-one. The media have set him up as a hero and then kicked him in the arse.'

For a man who had just announced a vow of silence, that was an impressively loquacious beginning. And, sure enough, Alley in his usual bluff and forthright manner soon began to hold forth about the way in which Bird's Test career came to grief.

In retirement in Somerset, and ailing a little from heart trouble, he had always been quick with a gruff rebuke whenever the mood took him and was not about to change the habits of a lifetime.

As we have seen, Alley himself deserves a mention in any list of characterful umpires. He never quite fulfilled his ambition to play for Australia and, shortly after the Second World War, emigrated to England, where he played county cricket for Somerset as a robust middle-order batsman and medium-paced bowler. Upon his retirement in 1968, he became a colourful addition to the first-class umpiring list.

His Test umpiring career was brief – 10 Tests in all – as his enthusiasm for getting on with the action did not endear him to the powers-that-be. Woe betide any batsman failing to impress Alley. Too much scratching around at the crease and at the first appeal by a bowler there was every likelihood that the batsman would be banished to the pavilion. Sometimes, he might even have helped the victim on his way with a curse or two under his breath. Bill used to get impatient about things like that.

'Jim Laker was one of the first fellows who set Dickie up as a bit of a character, on the BBC,' Alley asserted. 'I told Dickie, you're getting an image and it will do you no good. All that stuff about how he used to walk halfway towards the boundary before he signalled his fours and sixes. Everyone else followed on and soon Dickie became a hero. Then it all went wrong, and there it was in no time at all – the boot up the arse.'

Alley is one of many who is adamant that it was new technology which hastened Bird's downfall. Alley only differs in that he retired from the umpiring panel more than 10 years ago and so is free from the petty TCCB restrictions which might allow the game to function more cosily but which also remove the right to free speech. That those involved in sport accept such stringent restrictions, and are willing to concede a basic liberty, remains astonishing.

'New technology was trouble for Dickie,' Alley said. 'Whenever a bloke put his foot in it, people would scream for the TV umpire to be brought in and eventually the authorities just caved in. I was against the camera from the start. Completely against. It took all the responsibility away from the bloke in the middle. It gives everyone a chance to sit in judgement. These days the poor bloody umpire is put under more and more pressure. I tell you, the way the game is going, before long there will be a box on every ground with two lights on it, and no umpires on the field at all. It's happening already. I told them that in Australia more than 20 years ago and they just laughed at me. Now they're beginning to wonder whether I'm right. The thing about this third-umpire business is that it's the bloke behind the TV set who has got most of the control. Yet the TV umpire doesn't even have to be on the official Test match panel. He's regarded as an inferior, yet he's the one with the power.'

Throughout the game's history, the most respected umpires could expect to gain in authority with every passing year. There came a time in middle age when their considerable esteem derived as much from their long years of service as the quality of their decisions. To suggest that their judgement might be on the wane was virtually unthinkable. Players could easily be accused of sour grapes, while other observers, before the coming of slow-motion playbacks, were in no position to judge. Few thought to openly question such symbols of authority.

Technology changed all that. This is the era of third umpires charged with ruling on marginal decisions with the aid of TV playbacks from assorted angles; of match referees empowered with wide-ranging disciplinary powers; of stump cameras and sound-effect microphones; of more critical media, revolving sightscreens, big screens, logos garishly painted on outfields, coloured clothing, players' agents, marketing whizzkids and corporate hospitality boxes in prime positions. What on earth has happened to the fraternal, if run-down, game that Bird first experienced on his playing debut for Yorkshire in the mid-1960s?

Nowadays, every umpire is vulnerable, and every reputation thrown open to doubt. Anybody with access to a television screen can debate the quality of an umpire's decisions. The more obsessive cricket nerds have been known to edge a run-out decision through frame by frame on the video in an effort to prove that an umpire is at fault. As Bird himself has bemoaned: 'We can all be experts in an armchair.'

For a while, TV commentators tried to remain above the argument, scrupulously responding to dodgy decisions with the mildest of disapproving noises. It was just not cricket's way to castigate the man in charge, however error-prone his performance might have been. But gradually the climate changed. Public pressure demanded a more candid approach. If the man or woman in the pub could complain about the unfairness of decisions, they expected the commentators to reflect their views. The rising popularity of one-day cricket, too, had sold cricket to a wider audience, seeking quicker and simpler gratification. If they thought an umpire committed a howler, they wanted their views underlined with more than a gentle tut-tut.

* * *

In Australia, by the end of the 1970s, Kerry Packer's Channel 9 had hastened the process. Controversy was now part of the package and, however much the traditionalists squealed, there was no turning back. Cricket was to be debated, not soaked up in respectful silence. Bird, as we know, possessed the skills to survive that trend, and his reputation was often enhanced in the process. If the TV replay occasionally proved him fallible, it also proved him far less fallible than others. If he tended to be a bit of a not-outer, especially where lbws were concerned, at least no-one could challenge his consistency. He was undoubtedly the world's leading umpire, and a great entertainer to boot. But the moment his powers began to wane, Bird's reservoir of public respect evaporated far more quickly than it would have done in an earlier age. In a world that demanded results – in schools, business and sport – immediate performance now counted for far more than reputation.

Faith in the old loyalties was still entrenched within the

TCCB. Umpires on the county circuit are marked over the season by the county captains and, as hard as the TCCB strove to keep the ratings private, Bird's position in the league table had not been consistently outstanding for several years. When umpiring representatives politely suggested that this should be taken into account when appointing Test umpires, a TCCB official allegedly retorted: 'What! Sack Dickie? He's an institution.'

At county level, impatience began to grow among his fellow umpires. Everybody had great affection for Bird and recognised his bottomless commitment to the game. But he was not the only first-class umpire with personal ambitions to satisfy. Young men had entered the profession in the belief that they, too, could achieve great things. Umpiring was no longer a safety-net for a few old pros fallen on hard times. By helping to raise its public profile, Bird had encouraged greater expectations among the next generation. When he was no longer the unchallenged number one, it was only to be expected that some of his colleagues would hanker after greater opportunity at Test level.

Matthew Engel argues that too much can be made of technology's part in Bird's decline. 'I don't accept that TV destroyed him, it merely made his decline more obvious,' he said. 'The word would have got around soon enough.' Scyld Berry, cricket correspondent of *The Sunday Telegraph*, also shies away from linking the start of Bird's regression to new technology. He began to wonder if Bird's impeccable standards were beginning to falter during the 1991 Lord's Test against Sri Lanka. Ian Botham's last Test wicket for England was a questionable affair, TV replays suggesting that it deflected through to wicketkeeper Jack Russell off Roshan Mahanama's thigh pad. Botham's appeal was emphatic and, after a lengthy delay, umpire Bird ruled in his favour. 'Both's last 10 Test wickets were a bit of a struggle,' Berry said. 'Sometimes they seemed to be won by the sheer force of his personality.'

Nevertheless, without the pressures fuelled by new technology, it seems probable that Bird would have been allowed to continue on the Test circuit, irrespective of whether or not his judgement was as acute as before, until he reached retirement age at 65. That, after all, was a more gentlemanly, more compassionate way of doing things – and Dickie's popularity throughout the country was as strong as ever.

Umpires have long been aware of the threat of the TV camera. Barrie Meyer umpired alongside Dickie Bird in both the 1979 and 1983 World Cup finals. At that time, the BBC managed with far fewer cameras than are used today, the only camera behind the bowler's arm being situated in the Lord's pavilion. The match was then televised from only one end. That meant that while the umpire standing at the Pavilion End was filmed from behind, so allowing the camera to have a clear view of his lbw decisions, the umpire at the Nursery End was in the happier position of having the camera stationed behind the batsman, whose body often obscured where the ball had pitched, so leaving any lbw decision impossible to analyse.

Bird's and Meyer's walk out to the middle at Lord's for the start of the 1979 final between England and the West Indies was a happy affair, Dickie warmly congratulating 'BJ' on his appointment, giving him an uplifting reminder that they were the best two umpires in the world and wishing him all the best. Then, without further ado, he was off, striding up to the Nursery End before Meyer could blink. Not that he holds any grudges. 'They probably call it senior umpire's prerogative,' Meyer said. 'I should think that Tommy Spencer did the same thing to Dickie in 1975.'

However much he might feel that he was hounded by technology in his later years, Bird will reach retirement as convinced as ever that the umpire's role will never be entirely usurped by it. He does not share the awful vision of some of his colleagues – Alley among them – that one day a Test will be played without any dismissals being given on the field of play: 'We need electronic aids for the close run-outs and the close stumpings, but that is all,' Bird argues. 'I think umpires will be here until the end of time.'[37]

There was a time, though, when Bird's hostility towards electronic aids was much more marked. While the battle over their introduction was still being fought, he had rejected the suggestion that they might improve umpiring standards. 'I hope I never see them again on a cricket ground,' he said. 'They would be no use for lbws, because the height can only be judged by the umpire at the bowler's end. The umpire also has to consider where the bowler delivered the ball in the area of the crease and how much the ball did off the seam. I don't want to see the human element taken away. A machine would be no use for catches behind the wicket because you hear all sorts of noises out there when the keeper appeals. They would only be of use in close run-outs.

'But a top-class umpire does not make many mistakes in that area, you know. I never want to see those huge electronic scoreboards over here that they have in some Australian grounds. They cause trouble among spectators ... and they don't convey the different noises and the height of delivery. I think those screens are inflammatory. A third umpire would also be just a gimmick. What about the delays involved as the two umpires wait for the third man's decision up in the stands? It would look awful. What is wrong with simply taking the word of the umpires as they judge it with the naked eye?'[38]

Had anyone told Bird, as he took his first, faltering umpiring steps, that by 1993 a major cricket sponsor would seriously suggest equipping umpires with miniature TVs to assist with decisions, he would have said they were mad. But Reliance Industries, official sponsors of the 1996 World Cup, proposed just that. It deserved laughing out of court, and fortunately was, proving that cricket still retains some sanity. Bird was so flabbergasted he could say little other than that he was 'amazed'.

As Christmas approached in 1993, the ICC finally announced its commitment to the introduction of independent umpires. Partly for reasons of economy, and partly to allow some opportunity for advancement for home umpires, one umpire from a neutral country was to be appointed for each Test match to stand alongside a home umpire. The independent panel was to be 20 in number, but the initial announcement concerned only one name: Dickie Bird was to launch the system during Pakistan's series in New Zealand early in 1994.

All previous experiments with independent officials had been privately arranged by the cricket boards concerned. Now, thanks to a £1.1m sponsorship over three years by the National Grid, the implementation was to be worldwide. Prolonged discussions over the previous three years had convinced the ICC that the employment of two neutral officials would prove unpopular and unworkable, not only on financial grounds. Many English umpires are attracted to the professional county circuit by the hope of officiating in a home Test. Imagine the loss to Bird if he had never stood in a Lord's Test, his eyes misting over as the Queen advanced down the line of players towards him.

The independent panel was in keeping with several decisions taken by the ICC to combat cricket's faltering reputation for fair play. With the advocacy of a past chairman, Sir Colin Cowdrey, the hand of authority was strengthened with a code of conduct, a match referee empowered to act on disciplinary matters, and the advent of a third umpire.

Bird's ability to control players' behaviour remained unsurpassed, but many of his colleagues were experiencing greater difficulty. Barely a tour has passed in recent years without relations between the two sides being damaged because the visiting players perceive umpiring bias. Officials have also been subject to a combined assault from inflamed national passions and gamesmanship from batsmen who no longer walk and fielders who automatically appeal for every conceivable decision. Change was inevitable.

By virtue of his seniority, as well as his positive promotion of the game for nearly a quarter of a century, Bird was the obvious choice to launch the scheme. The subliminal message was that if Dickie was involved, it must be good for the game. Sir Colin was conscious of Bird's importance: 'It was never going to be easy to suddenly tell countries that the ICC was going to impose certain umpires in their home series. But Dickie had always been trusted and, wherever he went, he was sure to blend in. With England being the only Test-playing country in the northern hemisphere, he was also available to umpire throughout our English winter. He was very important to us, but he was never the sort to play the "Big I Am". At the heart of him, there was always a certain insecurity.

'Dickie had a wonderful way with him. His flaps were always under control; however excitable he got, his discipline never came into question. All this End Of The World Is Nigh stuff was a marvellous act as long as it didn't get out of hand. His umpiring style was unique, but I don't think he is necessarily the last umpire of personality. Each individual, having achieved a stature, can do his own thing. Even allowing for all the changes in the game, I still have faith in cricket's ability to produce characters. There has to be more humour in the game all round. That, I think, is the abiding memory of Dickie: he was able to laugh. No-one took the game more seriously than he did. No-one was keener to do his job well. Yet, at the heart of him, there was always laughter; his humanity was never very far away. That is the lesson that cricket should learn from him.'

Nigel Plews, another of England's four original members on the ICC panel, also recognised that Bird's involvement was vital for the scheme's success. 'Dickie was exactly what was needed,' he said. 'The sponsors, National Grid, needed a name to attract publicity so they were happy, and Dickie's reputation for fair-mindedness suited cricket, too. The whole concept of neutral umpires could not have been introduced as speedily or as successfully without him. Dickie's involvement gave everybody confidence.'

At 60, Bird must have been relieved that the authorities had given him his due, and he did not hesitate to give the scheme his full endorsement. 'Players seem to accept decisions better and get on with the game quicker if there is no suspicion of bias,' he said. 'I also think this system will help cut down on mass appealing, which has crept into the game.'

Such positive noises demanded a switch in attitude on Bird's part. He had long believed that the best alternative would have been to form an elite panel of eight umpires, irrespective of their nationality. He had not formerly had much enthusiasm for neutral umpires, believing that the removal of the incentive of standing in a home Test match could cause a dangerous shortage of top-class umpires throughout the world in years to come. It will be some years yet before that conviction has been tested.

'Whatever anybody says, all umpires are neutral,' he said in 1987. 'They are fair and honest men who give decisions as they see them. Cricket has always been a gentleman's game. Let's get on and play it. The only way round the problem would be to choose the best eight umpires in the world, wherever they are from. I don't care whether they are from Timbuktu. Those eight would do all the Tests around the world. Then you would have to pay them up to the standard of the players because of the intense demands placed upon them.'

Bird's underlying assumption, shared by many of his colleagues, was that most of the best umpires came not from Timbuktu but from England, where the presence of 18 first-class counties and a heavy summer programme necessitated the only group of full-time professional umpires in the world.

He had expanded on that view in 1993, saying: 'Without pushing my own claims or those of my English colleagues, it is fair to say that we maintain comfortably the highest standards. It would therefore be wrong to leave out some excellent umpires from England to accommodate less well-qualified men from elsewhere because this would mean a decline in the level of competence. It is surely no use having neutral umpires if they slip up because they lack the necessary background. Indeed, home crowds are not going to be very tolerant of a "foreigner" making mistakes, particularly if they happen to prove costly to their side.'

Bird went on to question overseas umpires' ability to handle the atmosphere of Test cricket, suggesting that only the Olympic Games rated as a bigger occasion. In reality, national pride would always prevent ICC delegates agreeing upon the identity of the best eight umpires in the world, irrespective of what country they represented. To assume that England would be invited to supply world cricket with a steady stream of officials sounded dangerously close to paternalism. It was an attitude doomed to fail.

Bird's ambitions for umpires' pay scales to rival those of the players also remained unrealised. The ICC failed even to equalise payments to umpires. Instead, for example, the Indian umpire S. Venkataraghavan received a substantially lower fee from the Indian Cricket Board than did Bird from the TCCB. The ICC argued that this took into account the different standards of living in each country and, furthermore, recognised that Indian players were also more poorly paid than their English counterparts. To equalise Venkat's payments might result in him earning more than the Indian players, which would obviously be unworkable.

What ultimately emerged was a workable compromise. England, in recognition of its reservoir of professional umpires, provided four umpires (the three named later were David Shepherd, Nigel Plews and Ken Palmer), with the other eight Test-playing nations nominating two each. There was to be no right of appeal by a Test nation against the independent umpire assigned by the ICC to stand in the series. In spite of predictable scaremongering – sections of the media raised the spectre of Shakoor Rana – it was an overdue step forward.

Time was short if the system was to be launched on schedule and, in mid-January 1994, I popped in to see Bird at White Rose Cottage. He was pacing around in more of a dither than usual. The carpet could not be seen for letters strewn haphazardly around the floor, he couldn't quite remember where he was, there was fruit loaf still to cut and he was sorry, but had he forgotten to pour the tea? Most agitating of all, his presence on the ICC's international umpiring panel had brought with it the obligatory form to complete. He had never been one to fill in forms; he was rarely able to sit down long enough.

'They want to know how much notice I would need to umpire a Test overseas,' he said. 'I don't need any at all. My bags are always packed. I could leave today.'

He was persuaded to answer '24 hours' if only for the milkman's sanity, but he would have been happier responding 'This very minute.' His devotion was extraordinary.

Bird umpired the first two Tests, beginning in Auckland on 10 February, with both matches resulting in comprehensive Pakistani victories. If Bird's 56th Test represented another satisfying milestone, it was not without embarrassment, as Richard Spencer reported for *The Daily Telegraph*: 'The first Test match to use the controversial "neutral umpire" system was marred yesterday by errors involving Dickie Bird, the doyen of cricketing officials. The Yorkshireman and his fellow umpire, Steve Dunne of New Zealand, miscounted the balls in an over no fewer than six times in the first two days of the New Zealand–Pakistan match. In a match already heading for the record books as 30 wickets fell in six sessions, Mr Dunne twice called five-ball overs, twice seven-ball overs and once allowed eight deliveries before handing the bowler back his cap. Mr Bird called "Over" after five balls during New Zealand's second innings.

'The errors, eventually pointed out by the two official scorers, are by no means the worst laid at the door of umpires in recent stormy Test history. But while most players have noticed an occasional discrepancy as umpires transfer their six pebbles or pennies from one pocket to the other, it is rare for it to be brought to official attention. Two years ago Philip DeFreitas bowled a four-ball over for England against New Zealand at Eden Park. And in 1963 John Sparling spun 11 deliveries down the wicket of the same ground against England when umpire Dick Short had problems with his hand counter after five balls and, instead of checking, decided to start again.

A complaint against Mr Bird, widely regarded as the world's best umpire, is a rare matter indeed. He was the almost automatic first selection for the new panel.'

It took David Richards, the chief executive of the ICC, to put matters into perspective. 'If a person makes an arithmetical mistake it doesn't matter which country he comes from,' he said.

But it was the 1995 English season that marked a watershed for Bird and, in particular, England's Texaco Trophy one-day international against the West Indies at the Oval. On more than one occasion, Bird seemed harassed by the authorities' insistence that all close run-out decisions be referred to the third umpire, whether or not the official on the field had any doubts in his own mind. This instruction sounded simple enough, an attempt to ensure that there were no unnecessary human slip-ups. If video evidence was available, then it stood to reason that it should be used as a safeguard whenever there was a close decision. But, for an umpire who had had a lifetime of making split-second judgements, and more often than not getting them right, it was a recipe for confusion. Instead of merely asking themselves, 'Am I sure whether that is out?' Bird and his colleagues now had to decide not only 'Am I sure?' but also determine whether, in the eyes of officialdom, they had a right to make the decision without the aid of video back-up. One slip, and media criticism would rain upon them.

The safest modus operandi was to refer decisions to the third umpire even when everybody on the field was convinced about the outcome. It has become a common sight for umpires to call in video evidence while casually informing a batsman that he did not make his ground. The judgement is rarely fallible. A lengthy delay then ensues, with much nodding and winking among the fielding side, and the batsman fearing the worst but forced to await the inevitable red light.

For an umpire with Bird's length of service to make the adjustment was perhaps more difficult than for someone starting out on their international career. An umpire with an outstanding track record was now expected to work in tandem with a machine which, by its very nature, questioned his judgement. There are many sixty-somethings in England who would rather get to their feet to change a TV channel than use a remote control, who are afraid of leaving a message on an answerphone in case it bites them, and who can never quite manage to tape the right programme on the video, unless their eight-year-old grandson happens to be close at hand. Technophobia is the most common ailment in the land.

Chris Campling, in *The Sunday Times*, emerged as one of Bird's fiercest critics. Following the one-day international at the Oval, he wrote on 4 June: 'First, Bird called on the third umpire to adjudicate on a run-out so obvious that the batsman, Graeme Hick, was well on his way to the pavilion before the replay confirmed it. Then Bird did not call on the camera to rule on a run-out appeal against Neil Fairbrother. Had he done so England's best one-day batsman would have been out by a foot. But he stayed, and shepherded his side to a winning total.'

Campling accepted that this was 'a rare blemish', but noted that Andy Roberts, the West Indies coach, had called the Fairbrother decision the turning point of the game. Richie Richardson, as befits such a chivalrous and civilised man, had refused to criticise Bird at all. According to Richard Little, the TCCB's media officer, Bird, who rarely watches replays for the sake of his sanity, did watch this one and was 'crestfallen'.

Media reproof for Bird's performance at the Oval was widespread. Paul Allott, on *Sky TV*, spoke of a 'monumental blunder'. Mike Selvey, in *The Guardian*, wrote: 'When Fairbrother had made only 29, Ambrose, in his follow-through, had booted the ball onto the batsman's stumps with, as the television replays confirmed, the player at least a foot short of his ground. But Dickie Bird, the square leg umpire, who has always prided himself on the accuracy of his judgement on close calls, gave the batsman the benefit. Bird, as he is entitled but unwise to do in this age, ignored the technology and made his own decision. But he got it wrong when he could have got it right. Furthermore, it was a totally inconsistent thing to do, for earlier, when Carl Hooper's direct hit from short third man had caught Hick at least four yards short of the crease and scarcely in the picture, Bird was signalling frantically for the replay even as the batsman continued his run towards the pavilion. It looked and was ridiculous.'

Selvey pointedly remarked that the Australian Darrell Hair had been taken to task by the ICC match referee, John Reid, in Australia the previous winter for not availing himself of the technology and making errors of judgement as a result. Reid was also the match referee that day at the Oval.

Campling's criticism went further. Indeed, he seemed to lose touch with reality when he suggested that Bird's 'mind was wandering' when the West Indies appealed for the Hick run-out and that he was not 'fully alert'. Quite what mystic powers allowed this 'fact' to be revealed is not known. He then fell back on the fallacious charge commonly laid by Bird's detractors over the years that 'Dickie Bird the media star has overtaken Dickie Bird the umpire.' Suffice to say that those who have known him since childhood reject the claim out of hand. How he is today is how he has always been.

When the TCCB introduced the third-umpire system in 1993 they gave the TV official the power to intervene 'if he can clearly see something that those in the middle may not themselves have seen'. It was stressed at the time that they even had the power to suspend what TV evidence proved was a bad decision to allow a chance for it to be reconsidered. George Sharp, the duty third umpire, for whatever reason, was unable to help on this occasion.

TV had proved other umpires equally fallible, and will continue to do so. During Graham Gooch's match-winning century against Pakistan at Headingley in 1993 – one of the finest Test knocks of the modern era – he was seen to have been run out by about four feet. The umpire Ken Palmer was so convinced that Gooch had made his ground that he would not have called upon a third umpire to settle the doubts in his mind; he simply did not have any. In such cases, if technology was to be used, it had to be used with conviction: the third umpire had to have the right to intervene.

England, alone of the Test-playing nations, habitually equipped their umpires with walkie-talkies to ensure that they were not isolated from the decision-making process. Strenuous efforts have been made since then to persuade the ICC to standardise this sensible policy worldwide. Had Bird rapidly been made aware of the narrowness of the Fairbrother decision, he would still have had time to call for a playback.

The walkie-talkie system, admittedly, has had a few teething problems. Much thought is given to operating on a frequency that will not be picked up by spectators inside the ground. Things have been known to go awry, however. During one match at the Oval, a London taxi driver rang in to say how much he was enjoying the umpires' comments that had been coming loud and clear into his cab throughout the day.

There were those who felt, in their heart of hearts, that all this technological assistance would end in tears. Michael Parkinson, a close friend of Bird's for nearly half a century, wondered sympathetically: 'God knows what it will do for Dickie Bird when he starts hearing voices in his ear.'

To return to Chris Campling, Bird's chief critic. In *The Sunday Times*, Campling had also accused him of mistakes in a Benson & Hedges Cup quarter-final on 30 May 'at Old Trafford'. Not as big a mistake as his own. Bird had actually stood at Canterbury, and predictably he brought in his own 'third umpire' by taking legal advice. *The Sunday Times*, threatened by legal action, hastily apologised.

But Bird's performance in the quarter-final at Canterbury had, indeed, not been without controversy. Paul Weaver, in *The Guardian*, recorded during his report of Kent's clash with Middlesex: 'Ealham was run out, a close call by Dickie Bird which was later vindicated by the television replays. The slow-mo was not so generous to Bird when Angus Fraser claimed to have Steve Marsh caught behind. Fraser thought the ball had gone off Marsh's glove, but when Bird refused to uphold the catch, the furious bowler advanced down the wicket and exchanged heated words with the batsman.'

Things had markedly changed since the early days of slow-motion replays. Often, the BBC would not re-run a replay which showed the umpire was in error, for fear of undermining his authority. If they did so, the evidence was often accompanied by the most understated and obscure remark. Twenty years on, if the umpire made a balls-up, everybody knew about it. It was a harsher, less respectful, world.

When England went 1–0 down to the West Indies after losing the first Test at Headingley, consideration of Bird's unconvincing start to the summer seemed unavoidable. The demands of new technology seemed to have put him in a muddle. Even so, to question his judgement did seem like violating a national monument.

Roundly criticised for not calling for a TV replay in the Texaco Trophy for Fairbrother, Bird had reacted by calling up the replay facility at Headingley to confirm that Brian Lara had made his ground. From any vantage point on the ground, there did not seem the remotest possibility that he had been run out and when the replay confirmed that Lara was home by the width of the crease, hoots of derision sounded in the Headingley press box. In *The Guardian*, I offered the following comments: 'Eccentricity should be valued and Bird has been one of English sport's treasures for more than two decades, an umpire in a perpetual flap, twitching away as if he has given refuge to an army of worker ants. The judgement upon whether his eccentricity is acceptable has always rested upon two considerations. Firstly, is it entirely natural, and not an attempt at self-promotion? In Bird's case, it assuredly is. Secondly, has it interfered with his ability to do the job. Until recently it has not – he has been widely praised as the best umpire in the world. But when eccentricity tips from quaintness to aberration, it is time reluctantly to wonder whether international retirement, after 62 years and 62 Tests, might soon be the wisest option.'

In making those observations, it was erroneously suggested that Bird's failure to call for the TV umpire to adjudicate on the Fairbrother run-out had occurred at Lord's, not (as had been the case) at the Oval. Proof, as if it was needed, that not only umpires make mistakes. Bird penned a hurt reply to *The Guardian*. However vexatious the affair was, the essential point still seemed valid. Instructions on the use of TV replays were not making his life any easier.

Kevin Mitchell picked up the theme in *The Observer* on 18 June. 'How do you phone Harold 'Dickie' Bird, one of nature's endangered species, and ask him if he thinks he is, well, past it?' he asked. 'With severe doubts about your humanity and the worth of your calling, for a start.' Taking a lead from Linford Christie, Mitchell reminded us that 'national icons should be treasured not buried'. He was right. Bird had been one of the most popular and acclaimed sporting personalities in Britain for the past 25 years and deserved the warmest of send-offs. But that he recognised the need to wind down while that respect and affection remained seemed absolutely crucial. Mitchell went on:

'If he goes, it will be the technology that he initially resisted that did for him. And this would be cruel. Until the third umpire was introduced, cricket had relied on the integrity of players and officials alike to conduct themselves properly, with decisions taken, largely, without demur. It was the very essence of the game, although only the blind would contend that skulduggery did not lurk in the hearts of some. You could never accuse Bird of harbouring even the slightest dark thought. He is smiling, boyish innocence itself. His umpiring has invariably been cautious, no bad thing before the dreaded camera invaded the scene to lend certainty to borderline situations. The pressure now is greater than it ever was, not less; the finger stays down, the replay comes up ... and the nation sits in judgment from the comfort of a few million armchairs. That is some hanging party.'

By the time of Australia's home Test series against Pakistan in late 1995, the dwindling of Bird's talents was being openly discussed. It was an unwelcome shock after so many years as the unquestioned number one, but for the most part he was beginning to bear it in philosophical mood. He was coming to terms with the recognition that he was far from infallible. It was as if he had begun to realise that his international days were numbered.

In an interview with Martin Blake, of the highly-respected *Melbourne Age*, he insisted that a heightened awareness of umpiring mistakes had not lessened his enjoyment of the game: 'You take the job on and you know that you are in a no-win situation. When you make a mistake everybody knows and it's blown up. But you have to live with that. When you take the job on, you know that it's not all going to be rosy. If you make a mistake, the most important thing is the next ball. You have to get that mistake out of your head if you can. But it's not easy. I've never watched replays. If I did I'd go crazy. People make mistakes in all walks of life, don't they? In any case, you can't do anything about it once you've made the decision.'

Even consideration of the rise in concerted, mass appealing – which, at its most extreme form, is tantamount to games-manship – only drew from Bird a sagacious shake of the head: 'It's one thing that's changed in the game, with the massive appealing. But there's nothing to stop them, because there's nothing in the laws against it. It puts a lot of pressure on the umpire, but there's nothing you can do.'

Neither did he take refuge in the complaint that he was a victim of worsening on-field behaviour. Dickie's loyalties towards the players remained true to the last.

'Is player behaviour getting worse?' Blake asked.

'I wouldn't say that. The only change I see is the massive appealing. You get the odd situation that crops up, but you just need to have a whisper in their ear occasionally.'

Umpiring standards were inconsistent in Australia throughout their 1995/6 summer, but the focus did not fall on Bird. The home press were largely concerned with the inconsistent performances of some of their own umpires. Wasim Akram, Pakistan's captain, controlled his resentment after the second Test in Hobart and remarked only that he would be 'sending the ICC a very long report'. After Pakistan suffered further debatable decisions in Sydney (a match that, nevertheless, they won), Wasim referred to another ICC report. 'And this time it will be even longer,' he smiled.

The ICC's continued failure to standardise the third-umpire system in all Tests left the umpires in an invidious position. Bird umpired with walkie-talkies in England, but not in Australia, an inconsistency which the world's top officials should not have had to tolerate. The weakness of the Australian system became all too apparent when the TV replay system in the third umpire's room broke down during the Hobart Test. Unaware of the problem (to expect the umpires to keep a perpetual check on a small white light 100 yards away amid a tensely-fought session was clearly absurd), Bird at one point summoned a video playback when none was officially available, even thought TVs were re-running the incident all over the ground. Fortunately, when the decision was tossed back to him, Bird's judgement was impeccable.

That Bird should experience culture shock in India was understandable, but there were times when he came close to it in Sydney. Steve Randell's first overseas umpiring assignment had been alongside Bird in the Atherton 'ball-tampering' Test, a match played in soaring temperatures.

'Well, the coats are coming off, eh, Dickie,' Randell had said. 'All we have to sort out is whether we're going to wear ties.'

'What!' exclaimed Bird, as if traumatised. 'You can't do that. This is Lord's!'

Randell was delighted to find the boot on the other foot in Sydney, little more than a year later. With temperatures in the 30s, Randell announced that the umpiring coats would not be needed.

Bird looked at him in horror. 'But where am I going to put my counters?' he asked. 'If I put them in my trouser pocket, I'll lose 'em. I'll never know how many balls have gone. You're going to have to help me out.'

Peter Roebuck, one journalist who saw all that series, felt that Bird's Test career had naturally run its course. 'Past performances can buy you time, but they don't buy you the right to carry on for ever. Visiting teams welcomed him to the end, but there is always a new generation of players who understandably judge you on your ability rather than your reputation. History only has so much value for them. Dickie's confidence was slipping. For every umpire, the time comes when they stop seeing what their eyes reveal, or hearing what their ears tell them.'

Bird, however, had good reason to pride himself in his man-management skills in Australia. A Test series that had threatened to be one of the most savagely-fought for years, following Australia's bribery allegations against the former Pakistan captain Salim Malik, passed off peacefully. The part he had played in maintaining order should not be under-estimated. In fact, cricket was most discredited long after Bird – the players' man – had returned to England. In the Melbourne Test over Christmas, the Australian umpire, Darrell Hair, assured himself of fleeting fame by calling Sri Lanka's off-spinner Muttiah Muralitharan for throwing.

In the technological age, when it was constantly impressed upon umpires that they must use video assistance to determine run-outs, the pretence was ridiculously maintained that an umpire could fairly judge the legality of a bowler's action without recourse to the cameras. It was an appalling charade. Hair proudly believed he was just doing his job and that he deserved credit for his courage in addressing a long-recognised problem. But there must have been better ways of going about things than this, especially considering the intense media pressures of the 1990s. Bird, a deeply sensitive man, could not have been so merciless.

However much the umpires, with the assistance of the ICC, had privately studied video film before the Sri Lankan series, and however long Muralitharan had been under suspicion, to call him in the middle of a Test match was a compassionless act. Sri Lanka's subsequent explanation, supported by medical evidence, was that Muralitharan's bent elbow was due to a deformity from birth, and that it remained locked in position throughout his action. If that was the case, his action was legal. The explanation took both the umpire and the ICC by surprise.

When throwing became a contentious issue in the 1950s, warnings had been given as to the difficulty of the task facing umpires. Tom Smith, secretary of the Association of Cricket Umpires, produced a pamphlet in which he stressed that wrist movement or bent arm at delivery did not necessarily mean that an action was illegal.

A new system was overdue. Far more acceptable would have been an official ICC enquiry, at which reservations could have been raised in an even-handed manner and the player's defence considered. Only then should further action have been contemplated, and only then with the official assistance of video slow-motion. Bob Thoms, England's leading umpire a century ago, and one of the more unobtrusive officials, certainly felt that way. 'We are not going to do anything,' he insisted during one allegation of throwing. 'The gentlemen must do it.' Bird would doubtless concur.

It was while the claims and counter-claims regarding Muralitharan's action were at their height that Bird announced his international retirement. In such an atmosphere, the loss of cricket's supreme man-manager – kind-hearted, magnanimous yet invariably firm – was felt more keenly than ever.

10

A Clean Living

'I only ever think about cricket. I just worry that when I pack up I'll be dead in 12 months'

— Dickie Bird

LIST the various scandals that have afflicted cricket during Dickie Bird's career and, like most walks of life, it has been visited at one time or another by the Seven Deadly Sins. And a few more besides. But listen to the world's most famous umpire and the game is still blessed with principle and probity. Having spent a quarter of a century patrolling cricket's vices, Bird is forever eager to proclaim its virtues.

White Rose Cottage, his 17th-century home in Staincross, on the outskirts of Barnsley, is a temple to the game. It is a schoolboy's bedroom which has long outgrown itself, with cricket photos and memorabilia scrambling for every scrap of space. If there is an ornament or decoration that has no cricketing connotation, then it is not immediately apparent, having had the sense to hide itself quietly away as if recognising that it does not really belong. 'I'm awfully sorry, you probably don't remember me, I'm just a simple vase from Torquay. I really don't know much about cricket, never been interested in it, to tell you the truth. What's that, who is the third cricketer from the left, meeting the Queen? I know it's terrible, but I really don't have the faintest idea. Sorry, cricket's never really been my cup of tea. I've always been more interested in flower arranging. Look, if no-one can find any flowers to put in me, perhaps it might be better if I was going.'

Cricket has provided Bird with a satisfying and fulfilling life, but those who do not share his obsession might find cause to wonder whether it has also provided him with a substitute for living. There is little to suggest a rival interest. He likes a good tune but, as for reading, he cannot sit down long enough to pass the fly leaf. Cricket has been his infatuation and, as such, there has been no room for anything else.

'I only ever think about cricket,' he has said. 'I just worry that when I pack up I'll be dead in 12 months.' A contented and harmonious retirement, searching for a broader meaning to life, will not easily be put on the agenda. Bird's fears bring to mind the words of Fran Lebowitz: 'There is no such thing as inner peace. There is only nervousness or death.'

In his front room there are more than 100 photographs depicting a lifetime of cricketing memories. There are portraits, cartoons, decanters, even a tapestry. Dennis Lillee's Australian tour tie usually takes pride of place, along with a framed invitation to meet the Queen and a menu detailing a lunch (quail's eggs followed by venison) taken with the Prime Minister, John Major, at Chequers. A patriotic and unquestioning man, he takes an uncomplicated pride in them all. Every inch of wall is filled by a memory. In other circumstances, it might seem ostentatious, but that is not the case with Bird. It speaks partly of pride in his achievements and partly of companionship, a constant reminder of the friendships he has enjoyed. His keepsakes are the crutch of a deeply insecure man.

'I come home and I go to the letterbox and the mail is knee-deep,' he said. 'I answer every letter, sent to me from all over the world. But it would be nice to turn to someone to talk about different things and someone to lay my shirts out and ties and for someone to cook me a meal occasionally. Things like that. Probably, to a certain extent, I am lonely.'[39]

Other home comforts are lacking. He is no cook (he relied too long upon his mother's home cooking for that) and has never had any inclination to learn. He can take a peculiar pride in the bareness of his kitchen cupboards, throwing open the doors with gusto to reveal, more often than not, little more than a few tea bags and a couple of tins. In the cricket season, he exists upon cricket ground fare: pie and chips in the 1970s, salads in the '80s, pasta in the '90s. When at home he prefers to nip down to the Talbot for a pub lunch and, on his way home, stop off at the local butchers for a couple of sandwiches, to be eaten in front of the telly with a cup of tea. He is a fellow of humble tastes. His old mate, Jack Birkenshaw, is reminded of Bird's culinary habits every time he catches a glimpse of one of his more seasoned sports jackets. 'He makes a habit of picking up a couple of sandwiches from a cricket ground kitchen for his tea,' Birkenshaw said. 'At Old Trafford one day, he collected a piece of meat that looked a bit bloody, wrapped it in a couple of pieces of kitchen roll and put it in his pocket. It wasn't long before the blood began to seep into his jacket pocket. The last time I saw the jacket, you could still see the stain. He won't be eating beef now, though, won't Dickie, not with the BSE scare. In fact, that probably explains it: he's probably had BSE for years.'

On one diverting visit, in the mid-1980s, Bird managed to rustle up for me a piece of fruit loaf and a cup of tea which he fretted about constantly because someone had once written that he made the worst cuppa in South Yorkshire. We then adjourned to his local, where a white sheet was removed from one of the tables in the lounge and we had lunch surrounded by painters and decorators.

'The only other food I've got in the house is this piece of cheese,' he said on that occasion, pointing to the corner of the room. 'It's in that trap. I've got mice. I heard them three months ago, but I've never managed to catch one. I've left the cheese down all this time. Do you think it will be all right? They say that the older the cheese becomes, the more the mice are attracted to it. Should I keep it down a bit longer, or do you think I should buy another piece?' It seemed advisable to turn down the cheese.

Dickie frets about security, just as he frets about everything else, and even the security grilles are cast in the shape of interlocking cricket bats. If a burglar ever did breach the outer defences of White Rose Cottage, it is easy to imagine that he would be immediately assaulted by 100 bouncing cricket balls emerging from the walls, struck over the head by a robot wielding a Duncan Fearnley, and rained on from a great height before being given out by the shadowy figure of an umpire dressed in a characteristic white cap.

And soon will come the end as, in one form or another, it must come to all of us. During his last overseas Test series, Pakistan's tour of Australia in late 1995, Bird conceded that life after umpiring was his 'big worry'.

'I've been married to cricket,' he said. 'I've given my life to the game. That's why I never married, because I didn't think it would work. I've lived out of a suitcase since I was 19 years old and signed for Yorkshire. Cricket is my wife. If I've had any regrets it's about not having a family, because if I'd had a lad what played cricket that would have given me a lot of pleasure. I hope when I retire I can find something within the game. Maybe as a Test match referee.'[40]

And cricket *has* been his wife: a wife who has won his unceasing affection and admiration, dominating his every thought from the moment he first set eyes upon her; a wife who has prized him one moment, and had cause to scold him the next; a wife who has squeezed from him every emotion – joy, distress, hope and fulfilment; a wife whom he could love with the same passion and intensity at the end as the beginning. This has been far more than a warm and comforting relationship, it has had the infatuation of a first love.

Michael Parkinson once wrote: 'To say Dickie Bird loves cricket doesn't get anywhere near describing exactly what he feels for the game. It's a bit like saying that Romeo had a slight crush on Juliet or Abelard had a fancy for Héloïse. The game consumes his life and defines its horizons. It shapes the very posture of the man. Like a tree bent and moulded by the prevailing wind, so the curve in Bird's spine, the hunch of his shoulders, the crinkled eyes as he inspects the world, have been sculpted through a lifetime's dedication to cricket.'[41]

Bird has lived a bachelor's life. If he ever came close to marriage, it was while he was coaching in Johannesburg in the early 1960s. He has always been reluctant to talk about it, possessing the old-style morality that insists that sexual relationships are a private affair. But bachelorhood has been a topic that his interviewers have frequently raised as the long, lonely days of retirement approach. He offered a rare insight as his Test career drew to a close:

'She was the one. I was very, very close to marriage. She was a beautiful girl, blonde, with shortish hair, tall, very educated. She was studying Afrikaans and psychology at Wits University. Most importantly, she also liked cricket. We spent evenings together, but then the big problem was that I had to come back to England for the summer cricket season. There were so many obstacles and I couldn't see how it could work. She said she would travel with me; but you never know, do you? If you're in sport and living out of a suitcase, you can't be fair to a woman. Probably she pressed marriage more than I did. Underneath, I never really thought it would work. I was being honest about it, and all I could see in front of me was cricket, cricket, cricket.

'We said cheerio [in 1964] and that was it. I never saw her again. She understood the situation, and it would never have worked. Well, I don't think so. I have given all my life and everything to cricket, and I mean that in all sincerity. I've seen so many divorces in sport, when people are living away from home, and I don't want anything like that to happen to me. I worry so much that it would have eaten me away.'[42]

South Africa, where he coached regularly for more than a decade, also became a second home. Dickie coached in Johannesburg and stayed with Cippy and Irene Smith, who ran a market-gardening business. According to Don Wilson, who also became friendly with the family, 'They treated Dickie like another son, doing all his washing and cooking his meals.' Apartheid was still firmly rooted, and much of the coaching was among the white elite, but it was Bird who was Wilson's right-hand man when they took the first forays into the Soweto township to launch a multiracial coaching scheme that many had warned was foolhardy and doomed to failure. Facilities were non-existent, and the enthusiastic, barely-dressed children understood nothing about the game, but with perseverance the first steps were taken. Bird had played a small part in the development programmes which were to form the basis of South Africa's attempts to be re-admitted as a Test nation.

Bird has regularly voiced regrets at his wandering lifestyle, often talking of having to live life out of a suitcase, and admitting his creeping sadness that he had not had a son, someone to watch growing up and playing local cricket in his beloved South Yorkshire. If he has had pangs about never marrying, his outlook has never changed – he has remained convinced that it would have been incompatible with his cricketing life. Commitment, in his eyes, must be total if it is to mean anything. He remains an old-fashioned romantic, a man who can be moved to tears by Barbra Streisand or Nat King Cole. His fondness for Nat King Cole's 'When I Fall In Love' was particularly notable, if only for a lyric which seemed to capture the course that his life had taken.

'In a restless world like this is, love is ended before it's begun...'

At Worcester one teatime, his umpiring colleague, John Hampshire, decided to take him in hand (well, there was nothing else to do at the time) and told him it was high time he got married. Dickie sat there, twiddling his hair ('like Doubting Thomas out of the old *Dandy*,' says Hampshire) and agreed that his mother often used to tell him the same. 'There must be loads of widowers, dowagers, even young lasses, seeking a wealthy fellow like you,' Hampshire continued. 'You're famous, you're funny and you're loving. Get yourself a dog and some carpet slippers and sit by a roaring log fire.' Dickie nodded – not only his mother but his sister had told him the same thing, too. By that time, the two umpires were on their way back to the middle with the conversation still in full swing, Dickie on his way to the Cathedral End, Hampshire to the Pavilion End. Such is the way of Dickie Bird that there had to be a punchline to bring the conversation to a close, a line that would transport a semi-serious conversation back into the land of the surreal.

'Anyway, ah'll nivver get married,' shouted Bird (by this time the umpires were many yards apart). 'I'm frightened. Everyone's got Aids.'

'What?' cried Hampshire, nonplussed. 'Everyone? Even me and my lass?' Play resumed with several fielders looking more than a little perplexed.

That story is reminiscent of a letter sent a few years ago to *The Bangkok Post* which proposed that cricket should be enthusiastically promoted as a defence against the HIV virus. Just in case his logic was not immediately clear, the correspondent explained that: 'Cricket-playing nations are only capable of a limited amount of sexual activity.'

The Hampshires, also being natives of South Yorkshire, have regularly entertained Bird over Christmas. 'He was guaranteed to liven up Boxing Day morning,' said Hampshire. 'He would phone about three times to check when he was expected to arrive, and then he would pitch up around 8.30 in the morning while half the village was still asleep. He'd grab a pork pie and mince pie from the hallway on the way in and kiss all the family on the cheek, leaving them covered in crumbs. I'd take him down to the pub at lunchtime and it was as if the turn had arrived. He'd have a couple of Guinnesses and everybody would be in uproar listening to him. It's always a pleasure to have him. When he packs up, I'm sure there will be endless people wanting to wine and dine him. He'll never be sat there twiddling his thumbs. He might sit there twiddling his hair a bit, mind you.'

Bird's love affair with cricket has known no bounds. It has supported him financially, socially and spiritually. He is a practising Methodist, and prays every day, but even then cricket intervenes: on match days, he jokes, he always kneels by the side of his bed and asks to be spared rain and bad light. He has not been averse to using his religious beliefs to his advantage now and again on the field. 'I say to them, I'm a churchgoer, I go to church. I want you to be honest with me, young man, did you catch that fairly and cleanly? Because the Lord is watching us.'[43]

Quizzed about his lifetime's obsession with the game, about his private and solitary life as an unmarried man, he almost invariably thanks cricket for offering him 'a clean living'. It can sound almost prim and proper, and reveals a man who is naturally more at home in the more dignified and reticent morality of the 1950s. He even prefers to do daily exercises in the privacy of his bathroom. Not for Dickie a lycra tracksuit and an annual subscription at the local gym. You never know who you might meet.

His gratitude for cricket's promotion of 'a clean living' has its base in his Methodist upbringing, although such a refrain would have sounded distinctly odd to some of his most famous predecessors. William Clarke, the great Nottinghamshire stalwart, was 57 when he finally retired as a player but reports suggest that his drinking skills remained daunting for a good deal longer. Bird makes do with an occasional glass of stout, or glass of red wine, does not smoke and, during the summer, it is often lights out by 10.30 pm.

His was not a wealthy upbringing. For many years the family lived on a council estate in the New Lodge Estate in Barnsley. Dickie was accepted as a first-class umpire shortly after the death of his father and he remained at home with his widowed mother until her own death a decade later, moving a few miles up the road to Staincross only in the mid-1970s. Both his parents warned him against the perils of smoking, drinking and loose women.

'You can have all the friends in the world, but your mother is your best friend,' he states. 'She will never let you down.' He worshipped and respected both his parents and is saddened to believe that such devotion is less common today. Although he has been an irregular churchgoer, he had no choice but to attend Sunday School as a boy and the Methodist faith drummed into him during childhood has remained strong. He is proud of the fact that John Wesley reputedly once slept at White Rose Cottage. Like Wesley, he believes in thanking God for the gifts that he has been granted.

His respect for religion, for history and for cricket was illustrated at a memorial service in Wombwell, on the outskirts of Barnsley, to mark the centenary of the birth of Roy Kilner in 1990. Kilner, a gifted all-rounder, was one of Yorkshire's most popular cricketers, much praised for his charm, graciousness and generosity. White roses were laid on Kilner's grave at Wombwell cemetery, and Bird made a point of escorting Kilner's two elderly sisters to the graveside.

'For whatever reason, Dickie hadn't had an invitation,' recalled Jack Sokell of Wombwell Cricket Lovers' Society. 'He could easily have stayed at home and ignored us, but he rang up and asked if he could attend. He cares deeply about such things. He is far more than just a joker.'

Bird remains deeply wedded to the Barnsley area. His fame ensures that he is besieged by appeals for help, but he assists whenever and wherever he can, fulfilling speaking engagements, for example, to raise money for the town's homeless and for other good causes. He has never had an agent – never wanted one – and laboriously replies to each letter by hand. Letters are often strewn around the living room, his carpet operating as one huge in-tray. Cleaning and tidying are the province of his sister, Marjorie, who is a source of comfort for him and who can be relied upon not to interfere with his idiosyncratic filing system. If his socks happen to be buried between a letter from his bank manager and the milk bill, so be it; it is too late to change now. Marjorie, who has never quite understood his preoccupation with cricket, has described his life in Barnsley as being that of a recluse.

He has been so deeply attached to his profession that one wonders whether he will one day choose the course taken by Harry Bagshaw, the Derbyshire umpire, who was buried in 1927 in his white umpire's coat with a cricket ball in his hand.

With Bird's announcement of his international retirement, it was not long before the media began to speculate whether a late romance could be in the offing. *The Times* diary, in particular, could not resist the temptation to fill a few column inches:

'Now that Dickie Bird has decided to retire from Test cricket, is he ready for a romantic fixture? Dickie, a bachelor, has always maintained that umpiring all over the world has made marriage impossible. But after admitting in a TV interview that he was often lonely, he received three proposals of marriage and dozens of invitations to dates.'[44]

On the field, he has been the butt of at least one fairly basic sexual joke. The occasion was the 1990 Trent Bridge Test between England and New Zealand. It was Saturday evening, with only a remote prospect of further play, but umpires Bird and Hampshire were making a show of checking their light meters out on the square to prevent the natives getting restless. It was the first time that umpires had been issued with walkie-talkies and Allan Lamb could not let such a historic moment pass without another prank. Lamb borrowed the walkie-talkie of the third umpire, Alan Jones, who was in the England dressing room at the time, and rang the umpires to ask if they wanted a cup of tea. Jones duly arrived in the middle bearing two cups of tea on a tray, whereupon Bird discovered that someone had slipped a condom into his drink. Cue the punchline about not having used one of those things since 1960-something and much merriment all round.

Paul Allott, one of Bird's 'Gorillas', also recalls the day that Dickie took a painful blow in the groin at Old Trafford. 'It happened on the very day that we had enlisted Sheena Storah as our physio,' Allott said. 'Dickie was making a terrible fuss, as usual, and had to be helped from the field. You would have thought he was going to die. He didn't know anything about a female physio. As soon as he was told not to worry, because Sheena would look after him, he made a dramatic recovery. He turned right around and was back on the field again within seconds.'

If Bird is prepared for such jollity within cricket's enclosed world, he retreats elsewhere from what he regards as 'bad taste'. Among his many celebrity appearances in the months after he had announced his international retirement was on *The Big Breakfast*, where he was horrified to discover that the transvestite comedian Lily Savage planned to interview him, as is his custom, in bed.

Bird was having none of it. It might have been his Methodist beliefs, it might have been his own brand of morality, it might have been a certain prudishness. It might also have been that his single life had left him particularly protective of his sexual reputation. Whatever the reason, the man who had never been able to resist a jape was assuredly not about to leap into bed with a bloke dressed in a big wig, nightie and lashings of make-up. Even Savage's protestations that such macho types as Frank Bruno had been game enough to share his mattress in front of a nationwide TV audience failed to move him. 'I still wasn't going to get into that bed with him.' said Bird. 'I said if he wanted to interview me he could do it like a man while I sat in a chair.'

Before too long, Bird will have ample time to sit in a chair –

too much time, in fact. Peter Roebuck expresses the thoughts of many when he contends: 'It will be a long retirement. He is essentially a lonely and private man who has needed to be loved within the game. It has been important to him to feel that warmth throughout his umpiring career. Outside the game, he will probably find a chill. I think he should stay in the game, whether it be schools umpiring, Minor Counties, running umpiring courses or public speaking. He has a lot to tell. Running a game is as much about taking individual decisions as knowing the laws. That's hard to coach. But he has chosen his time well to retire from international cricket. Just as David Boon recognised in Australia before the 1996 World Cup, there is a time to retire when you will go and still be loved. This was Dickie's time and I'm personally pleased that he recognised it. All those who care for him will say the same.

'The idea of carrying on umpiring until the age of 65 won't last. Umpiring will become a more cut-throat profession, and it should do. County players cannot – and should not – choose their time to retire and the same should apply to umpires. It is all part of English cricket's need to become more professional. If the game wants greater financial rewards then it must aim for high standards in all facets of the game.'

Bird himself once said: 'If I live long enough, I can see myself when it's all over just sitting on a bench and telling the tale.' That bench will always be full of people eager to listen. In a lifetime committed to the game he loved, Dickie Bird communicated a sense of joy. For all the angst and all the heartache, he lived life to the sound of laughter.

Chronology

Triumphs and Trivia

Born: Barnsley, 19 April 1933.
Educated: Raley Secondary Modern, Barnsley.
1948: Debut for Barnsley CC, Yorkshire League.
1956–1959: Yorkshire CCC, 14 first-class matches.
1960–1964: Leicestershire CCC, cap 1960, 79 first-class
matches.
1965–1969: Professional at Paignton CC (Devon).
Qualified as advanced coach. Coached at Plymouth College
and in Rhodesia and South Africa.
1969: Appointed as first-class umpire for 1970 English season
with A.G.T. Whitehead, in place of A.S.M. Oakman
(resigned) and E.C. Petrie (not re-engaged).
1970
May 2–5: First first-class match: Notts v Warwicks, Trent
Bridge (with David Constant).
May 9–12: Surrey v Yorks, the Oval (arrives early, stopped by
policeman while clambering over wall).

1971
July 28: Lancs v Gloucs, Old Trafford, Gillette Cup semi-final
   (Lancs win in near-darkness at 8.50 pm).

1973
July 5–10: Test (1): Eng v NZ, Headingley.
July 20: First one-day international: Eng v NZ, Old Trafford.
Aug 9–14: Test (2): Eng v WI, Edgbaston (Arthur Fagg
   protest).
Aug 23–27: Test (3): Eng v WI, Lord's (bomb-scare Test).

1974
June 6–11: Test (4): Eng v Ind, Old Trafford (cuts Sunil
   Gavaskar's hair in middle of session).
July 20: First domestic cup final: Benson & Hedges Cup:
   Surrey v Leics, Lord's.
Aug 22–27: Test (5): Eng v Pak, the Oval (Sarfraz Nawaz
   bowls beamer at Tony Greig).

1975
May 31–June 3: Derby v Lancs, Buxton (snow stops play).
June 21: World Cup final: Aus v WI, Lord's (robbed of white
   cap during pitch invasion).
July 10–14: Test (6): Eng v Aus, Edgbaston (retired with back
   injury on third day, replaced by A.S.M. Oakman, then by
   T.W. Spencer).
Aug 28–Sep 3: Test (7): Eng v Aus, the Oval (Dennis Lillee's
   sit-down protest over refusal to replace ball).
Sept 6: Gillette Cup final: Lancs v Middx, Lord's.

1976
June 3–8: Test (8): Eng v WI, Trent Bridge.
June 17–22: Test (9): Eng v WI, Lord's (Michael Holding
   bowls beamer at Tony Greig).
Aug 12–17: Test (10): Eng v WI, the Oval (stoppage for pitch
   invasion).

1977

June 16–21: Jubilee Test (11): Eng v Aus, Lord's (Packer circus approach).

July 16: Benson & Hedges Cup final: Gloucs v Kent, Lord's (announces Bird's 'no' to Kerry Packer).

July 28–Aug 2: Test (12): Eng v Aus, Trent Bridge.

Aug 17–26: Gillette Cup: Middx v Somerset, Lord's (six days trying to obtain result because of rain).

1978

June 1–5: Test (13): Eng v Pak, Edgbaston.

June 29–July 4: Test (14) Eng v Pak, Headingley.

Aug 24–28: Test (15): Eng v NZ, Lord's (light meters introduced).

Sep 2: Gillette Cup final: Sussex v Somerset, Lord's.

1979

June 23: World Cup final: Eng v WI, Lord's.

July 21: Benson & Hedges Cup final: Essex v Surrey, Lord's.

Aug 2–7: Test (16): Eng v Ind, Lord's.

Aug 16–21: Test (17): Eng v Ind, Headingley.

1980

July 10–15: Test (18): Eng v WI, Old Trafford

Aug 28–Sep 1: Centenary Test (19): Eng v Aus, Lord's (Bird and Constant attacked by MCC members angry at delayed start).

Sep 6: Gillette Cup final: Middx v Surrey, Lord's.

1981

June 9–11: Derby v Essex, Chesterfield (carried from field injured on successive days by Dallas Moir).

July 25: Benson & Hedges Cup final: Somerset v Surrey, Lord's.

July 30–2 Aug: Test (20): Eng v Aus, Edgbaston (Bob Willis bowls England to great victory).

Aug 27–31: Test (21): Eng v Aus, the Oval.

1982

June 24–28: Test (22): Eng v Ind, Old Trafford.

July 8–13: Test (23): Eng v Ind, the Oval.

July 28–30: Lancs v Warwicks, Southport (Warwicks put on 470 for fourth wicket and still lose by 10 wickets).

Aug 12–16: Test (24): Eng v Pak, Lord's (Constant suggests to Bird that they might have to suspend play because of Pakistan's questioning of decisions).

Sep 4: NatWest final: Surrey v Warwicks, Lord's.

1983

June 25: World Cup final: Ind v WI, Lord's.

July 14-18: Test (25): Eng v NZ, the Oval (Phil Edmonds, England left-arm spinner, warned for intimidation after bowling two successive bouncers at Richard Hadlee).

July 23: Benson & Hedges final: Middx v Essex, Lord's.

Aug 25–29: Test (26): Eng v NZ, Trent Bridge (Allan Lamb lets firecrackers off behind Bird's back).

1983/84

Apr 6–13: First overseas assignment: Asia Cup, in Sharjah.

1984

May 12: Benson & Hedges Cup: Scotland v Yorks, Perth (Bird calls two tea intervals after new regulations fail to reach him).

June 14–18: Test (27): Eng v WI, Edgbaston (Andy Lloyd's facial injury; Malcolm Marshall warned for intimidation).

July 26–31: Test (28): Eng v WI, Old Trafford.

Aug 8–10: Notts v Derby, Trent Bridge (youthful Devon Malcolm warned for intimidation in first over of match).

Aug 23–28: Test (29): Eng v SL, Lord's.

Sep 1: NatWest final: Kent v Middx, Lord's.

1985

Apr 27–29: Leics v Yorks, Leics (stands in snow).

June 27–July 2: Test (30): Eng v Aus, Lord's.
July 20: Benson & Hedges Cup final: Essex v Leics, Lord's.
Aug 1–6: Test (31): Eng v Aus, Old Trafford.
Aug 29–Sep 2: Test (32): Eng v Aus, the Oval.

1986
July 3–8: Test (33): Eng v Ind, Edgbaston.
July 24–29: Test (34): Eng v NZ, Lord's.
Aug 2–5: Somerset v Worcs, Weston-super-Mare (retires ill
    after first day, replaced by R. Thorne, A.G.T. Whitehead).
Aug 21–26: Test (35): Eng v NZ, the Oval.
Sep 6: NatWest final: Lancs v Sussex, Lord's.

1987
June 4 8: Test (36): Eng v Pak, Old Trafford.
July 11: Benson & Hedges Cup final: Northants v Yorks,
    Lord's.
Aug 5–7: Lancs v Northants, Old Trafford (Lamb's practical
    jokes).
Aug 20–25: MCC Bicentenary match: MCC v Rest of World,
    Lord's.

1987/88
Nov 4: World Cup semi-final: Aus v Pak, Lahore (Bird
    subsequently scrubbed from his fourth World Cup final
    because England qualify).

1988
May 23–24: Bird's 100th international: Texaco Trophy: Eng v
    WI, Lord's (talks about retirement then changes his mind).
June 2–7: Test (37): Eng v WI, Trent Bridge.
July 21–26: Test (38): Eng v WI, Headingley (the blocked-
    drain Test).
Aug 4–8: Test (39): Eng v WI, the Oval.
Sep 3: NatWest final: Middx v Worcs, Lord's.

1989
June 22–27: Test (40): Eng v Aus, Lord's.
July 6–11: Test (41): Eng v Aus, Edgbaston.
Aug 24–29: Test (42): Eng v Aus, the Oval.
Sep 2: NatWest final: Middx v Warwicks, Lord's.

1990
June 7–12: Test (43): Eng v NZ, Trent Bridge.
July 26–31: Test (44): Eng v Ind, Lord's.

1991
June 6–10: Test (45): Eng v WI, Headingley.
Aug 22–27: Test (46): Eng v SL, Lord's.
Sep 3–6: Notts v Middx, Trent Bridge (falls out with Notts'
   groundsman Ron Allsopp over under-prepared pitch).

1992
Aug 6–9: Test (47): Eng v Pak, the Oval (ball-tampering
   controversy).

1992/93
Oct 18–22: Test (48): Zim v Ind, Harare (first Test overseas;
   first Test as neutral umpire).
Nov 1–5: Test (49): Zim v NZ, Bulawayo (breaks Frank
   Chester's world record of 48 Tests; breaks one of worst
   droughts in Zimbabwe's history).
Nov 7–12: Test (50): Zim v NZ, Harare.
Apr 16–18: Test (51): WI v Pak, Port of Spain (with colleague
   Steve Bucknor sets record number of Test lbws).
Apr 23–27: Test (52): WI v Pak, Bridgetown.
May 1–6: Test (53): WI v Pak, St John's (withstands pitch
   invasion by two Antiguan clowns).

1993
June 3–7: Test (54): Eng v Aus, Old Trafford (Merv Hughes
   calls him a 'legend').

July 22–26: Test (55): Eng v Aus, Headingley.

Aug 31–Sep 3: Kent v Northants, Canterbury (calls back Graham Cowdrey).

Sep 4: NatWest final: Sussex v Warwicks, Lord's.

1993/94

Feb 10–12: Test (56): NZ v Pak, Auckland (officially launches ICC's independent umpiring panel).

Feb 17–20: Test (57): NZ v Pak, Wellington.

1994

June 2–6: Test (58): Eng v NZ, Trent Bridge.

July 9: Benson & Hedges Cup final: Warwicks v Worcs, Lord's.

July 21–24: Test (59): Eng v SA, Lord's (Michael Atherton cleared of ball tampering).

1994/95

Sep 28–Oct 2: Test (60): Pak v Aus, Karachi (Salim Malik, Pakistan captain, accused by three Australian players of offering bribes to throw Test).

Nov 18–22: Test (61): Ind v WI, Bombay.

1995

May 26: Texaco Trophy international: Eng v WI, the Oval (failure to call in TV umpire to adjudicate on Neil Fairbrother run-out appeal is widely censured).

June 8–11: Test (62): Eng v WI, Headingley.

July 27–30: Test (63): Eng v WI, Old Trafford (sun stops play).

Sep 2–3: NatWest final: Warwicks v Northants, Lord's (Northants incensed after Dermot Reeve survives Anil Kumble's lbw appeal and turns game in Warwicks' favour).

Nov 17–21: Test (64): Aus v Pak, Hobart.

Nov 30–Dec 4: Test (65): Aus v Pak, Sydney.

1996

Jan 12: TCCB announces that Dickie Bird will retire from international cricket in June 1996. His farewell Test, his 66th, to be the Lord's Test between England and India on June 20–24. The TCCB also confirms Bird's intention to continue to umpire in first-class cricket until he reaches retirement age at 65 in 1998.

Statistics compiled with the assistance of Robert Brooke.

References

1. Patrick Murphy, *Declarations* (Ringpress Books, 1989)
2. *ibid*
3. *ibid*
4. *The Sunday Telegraph*, 21 Jan 96: interview by Helena De Bertodano
5. *ibid*
6. *The Daily Telegraph*, 3 Mar 93
7. BBC 'Look North' documentary (1990), with Harry Gration
8. *The Sunday Express*, 22 Nov 87: interview with Pat Gibson
9. Dickie Bird with John Callaghan, *That's Out* (Arthur Barker, 1985).
10. *ibid*
11. Sunil Gavaskar, *Sunny Days* (Rupa & Co, 1976)
12. Simon Hughes, *From Major To Minor* (Hodder & Stoughton, 1992)
13. Dickie Bird and John Callaghan, *From The Pavilion End* (Arthur Barker, 1988)

14. Ian Botham (with Peter Hayter), *Botham: My Autobiography* (Collins Willow, 1994)
15. *The Melbourne Age*, 17 Nov 95: interview with Martin Blake
16. *The Daily Mail*, 2 Sep 95: interview with Alice Fowler
17. Dennis Lillee, *Lillee: My Life In Cricket* (Methuen, 1982)
18. BBC 'Look North' documentary (1990), with Harry Gration
19. *The Sunday Telegraph*, 1 Aug 75
20. Bob Taylor (with Patrick Murphy), *Standing Up, Standing Back* (Collins Willow, 1985)
21. *The Melbourne Age*, 17 Nov 95: interview with Martin Blake
22. Dennis Lillee, *Lillee: My Life In Cricket* (Methuen, 1982)
23. Geoffrey Boycott (with Terry Brindle), *Boycott, the Autobiography* (Corgi, 1987)
24. Dickie Bird with John Callaghan, *That's Out* (Arthur Barker, 1985).
25. Dennis Lillee, *Lillee: My Life In Cricket* (Methuen, 1982)
26. *ibid*
27. Malcolm Marshall (with Patrick Symes), *Marshall Arts: The Autobiography of Malcolm Marshall* (Macdonald Queen Anne Press, 1987)
28. Patrick Murphy, *Declarations* (Ringpress Books, 1989)
29. Trevor McDonald, *Clive Lloyd, The Authorised Biography* (Granada, 1985)
30. Ian Botham (with Peter Hayter), *Botham: My Autobiography* (Collins Willow, 1994)
31. Henry Blofeld, *The Packer Affair* (Collins, 1978)
32. *The Observer*, Jul 73: interview with Michael Carey
33. BBC 'Look North' documentry (1990), with Harry Gration
34. Dickie Bird and Brian Scovell, *Not Out* (Arthur Barker, 1978)
35. Christopher Martin-Jenkins, *World Cricketers: A Biographical Dictionary* (OUP, 1996)

36. Bill Bowes, *Express Deliveries* (Stanley Paul, 1949)
37. *The Sunday Telegraph*, 21 Jan 96: interview with Helena De Bertodana
38. Patrick Murphy, *Declarations* (Ringpress Books, 1989)
39. BBC 'Look North' documentary (1990), with Harry Gration
40. *The Melbourne Age*, 17 Nov 95: interview with Martin Blake
41. *The Daily Telegraph*, 3 Apr 93
42. *The Daily Mail*, 2 Sep 95: interview with Alice Fowler
43. *Desert Island Discs* (BBC Radio 4), with Sue Lawley, 7 Apr 96
44. *The Times*, 16 Jan 96: 'Diary'

Bibliography

Particular use has been made of the excellent British Newspaper Library in Colindale (free of charge) and various computer databases (highly expensive). The opportunity, once again, to raid Tony Woodhouse's extensive cricket library was much appreciated. Special thanks also to Stephen Thorpe for access to his as yet unpublished work on Cec Pepper.

Of the many books researched, the following proved especially useful:

Dickie Bird and John Callaghan, *From The Pavilion End* (Arthur Barker, 1988).
Dickie Bird and John Callaghan, *That's Out* (Arthur Barker, 1985).
Dickie Bird and Brian Scovell, *Not Out* (Arthur Barker, 1978).
Henry Blofeld, *The Packer Affair* (Collins, 1978).
Mihir Bose, *All In A Day* (Robin Clark, 1983).
Ian Botham (with Peter Hayter), *Botham: My Autobiography* (Collins Willow, 1994).

Mike Gatting (with Angela Patmore), *Leading From The Front* (Queen Anne Press, 1988).

Sunil Gavaskar, *Sunny Days: An Autobiography* (Rupa & Co, 1976)

Derek Hodgson, *The Official History Of Yorkshire County Cricket Club* (Crowood Press, 1989).

Simon Hughes, *From Minor To Major* (Hodder & Stoughton, 1992).

Allan Lamb and Peter Smith, *Lamb's Tales* (Allen and Unwin, 1985).

Dennis Lillee, *Lillee: My Life In Cricket* (Methuen, 1982).

Trevor McDonald, *Clive Lloyd, The Authorised Biography* (Granada, 1985).

Teresa McLean, *The Men In White Coats* (Stanley Paul, 1987)

Mike Marqusee, *Anyone But England* (Verso, 1994).

Malcolm Marshall (with Patrick Symes), *Marshall Arts: The Autobiography of Malcolm Marshall* (Macdonald Queen Anne Press, 1977).

Patrick Murphy, *Declarations* (Ringpress Books, 1989).

Patrick Murphy, *Ian Botham: A Biography* (Dent, 1988).

Jack Simmons (with Brian Bearshaw), *Flat Jack* (Macdonald Queen Anne Press, 1986).

E.E. Snow, *Leicestershire Cricket 1949 to 1977* (Stanley Paul, 1977).

Bob Taylor (with Patrick Murphy), *Standing Up, Standing Back* (Collins Willow, 1985).

Don Wilson (with Stephen Thorpe), *Mad Jack: An Autobiography* (Kingswood Press, 1992).

Acknowledgements

Many people, too numerous to mention, have kindly assisted in the provision of material for this book, but particular thanks are due to: Jon Agnew, Bill Alley, Paul Allott, Ron Allsopp, Jack Bailey, Kim Barnett, Greg Baum, Peter Baxter, Scyld Berry, Jack Birkenshaw, Arthur Bower, Keith Boyce, Geoffrey Boycott, Terry Brindle, Steve Coverdale, Sir Colin Cowdrey, Robert Craddock, Barry Dudleston, Matthew Engel, Ron Fenton, John Hampshire, Ashley Harvey-Walker, Ian Healy, Benny Hill, Ian Hislop, Derek Hodgson, John Holder, Dorothy Hyman, Barrie Leadbeater, Dennis Lillee, Jim Love, Vic Marks, Barrie Meyer, Pat Murphy, Doug Padgett, Michael Parkinson, Nigel Plews, Derek Pringle, Steve Randell, Dermot Reeve, Peter Roebuck, Mike Selvey, Don Shepherd, Jack Sokell, David Steele, Andy Stovold, Lt.-Col. John Stephenson, Stephen Thorpe, Jim Tucker, David Warner, Don Wilson, John Woodcock and Tony Woodhouse. Plus, of course, those who preferred to remain anonymous.

Index